RALPH JOHNSON

of Perkins & Will   BUILDINGS AND PROJECTS

RALPH

JOHNSON

of Perkins & Will   BUILDINGS AND PROJECTS

RIZZOLI
NEW YORK

First published in the United States of America in 1995 by
Rizzoli International Publications, Inc.
300 Park Avenue South, New York, New York 10010

Library of Congress Cataloging-in-Publication Data

Johnson, Ralph, 1948–
   Ralph Johnson of Perkins & Will : buildings and projects /
introduction by Robert Bruegmann.
     p.   cm.
    Includes bibliographical references (p.   –   ).
    ISBN 0–8478–1862–4 (HC). — ISBN 0–8478–1863–2 (PB)
    1. Johnson, Ralph, 1948– —Themes, motives. 2. Perkins & Will.
3. Architecture, Modern—20th century.   I. Bruegmann, Robert.
II. Title.   III. Title: Ralph Johnson of Perkins and Will.
NA737.J62A4   1995   95–4983
720′.92—dc20   CIP

Designed by Sisco & Evans Ltd., New York

Jacket illustration, endpapers, and title page:
International Terminal, O'Hare International Airport, Chicago, 1989–1993.
Photograph by Nick Merrick © Hedrick Blessing

Printed and bound in Singapore

Contents

Introduction URBAN ELEMENTS BY ROBERT BRUEGMANN

With some architects the connection between personal character and built work is immediately perceptible. Among Chicago architects one thinks of the taciturn solidity of Mies van der Rohe, and of his buildings, devoid of unnecessary gesture, almost puritanical in their reduction to basic elements; or of Frank Lloyd Wright, whose prodigious, exuberantly inventive buildings seem of a piece with his extravagant personal life and flare for publicity; or of Helmut Jahn's carefully polished aura and the sleek glossiness of much of his work. In these cases the architect's life seemed to have found outlet in the work, and the work contributed to the creation of a public persona.

The connections between Ralph Johnson's personality and work are harder to detect. Very little in his soft-spoken, apparently diffident manner suggests the personality that led to the creation of plans as intricately formal as that of Warsaw Community High School, elevations as elaborately textured as those of Perry High School, or spaces as sweepingly dramatic as the ticketing hall in the International Terminal at O'Hare International Airport. In fact, it is almost disconcerting that these buildings issued from an individual so lacking in obvious affectation. Little in Johnson's work, moreover, suggests a calculated attempt to create a personal signature. Although Johnson's buildings are distinctive and obviously related to one another, differences in programs and sites usually overshadow any obvious stylistic similarities.

In part this is due to the temperament of the architect. Unlike many of his more flamboyant colleagues, Johnson exhibits little inclination to open his personal life or psyche to public scrutiny. It is not that he is by nature solitary; he has been a familiar figure in the Chicago architectural world since he joined Perkins & Will in the late 1970s, and he enjoys hearing about the work of colleagues. For Johnson, however, architecture is not primarily an act of personal will. Like all architects he clearly is interested in expressing himself through the creation of form, and he recalls Paul Rudolph in his fascination—perhaps even obsession—with certain formal motifs. But while many architects are primarily interested in being "form givers" and become so attached to their creations that they sacrifice important programmatic needs, Johnson fairly consistently lets the program drive his designs. Unlike architects who make a quick jump from program to a single, overwhelming image, Johnson's entire design process is built on the careful accretion of functional units into an elaborate whole.

This surprisingly rare ability to let program drive design has proved key to the recent and rapid rise in the number and size of Johnson's commissions. At client meetings Johnson talks a great deal about program and very little about art, because that is how he expresses himself among his closest architectural colleagues.

Although he recognizes that a split between the taste preferences of architectural-world insiders and those of building clients and users is often unavoidable, Johnson has never accepted the modernist notion of the avant-garde that holds that the architect's ideas should necessarily collide with prevailing tastes. In fact, he sees his own role in finding common ground. How can he transform popular expectations into a design that is new, fresh, and marked by his personal touch, without losing the quality that makes the structure legible to the public? How does one draw on regional building types and traditions without stripping the work of its own original stylistic expression or borrowing literal stylistic elements?

This attention to the symbolic and social role of buildings brings Johnson into close affinity with a number of the architects whose work he most admires: Dwight Perkins, Eliel and Eero Saarinen, the Dutch master Willem Dudok, Livio Vacchini, Aurelio Galfetti, and others often grouped under the label of European rationalists. For each of these architects each building presented an opportunity to extend the city by forging incomplete fragments into new ensembles, repairing breaches in the urban fabric, or creating new fabric through a careful extrapolation from existing elements. Each believed that the architect was obliged to weigh heavily the expectations of citizens, clients, and users. At the same time, every new building by each was a critique of the city, amending its less successful aspects or those that could be made fresher and more exciting.

Johnson is one of the few American architects to plumb the spirit of European rationalism and not merely its stylistic mannerisms. But he tends to part company with many rationalists in his ready acceptance of a wide variety of possible urban models. In rejecting modernist ideas, many rationalists merely inverted them, remaining profoundly modernist in their belief in the architect as a social engineer, one who retains the final say in matters of taste. The rationalists' views of the city—for example, their disdain for loosely settled suburbs and the automobile that makes them possible—often are every bit as doctrinaire as those of the modernists they criticize. Johnson presumes less. He accepts the fact that to criticize effectively, the desire to reform or to impose one's own views must bow to affection for the object of reform, or at least to a tolerant understanding of it. Like Dudok, Johnson is not much interested in imposing his signature on the urban fabric or in reforming society as a whole, but rather in assembling elements to create a city at once familiar and exciting, richly varied yet systematic and coherent.

At first glance the work in this book appears to defeat any sustained effort at analysis. Johnson has emerged as a mature architect and a major figure in the American architectural firmament only within the last half-dozen years. Many of the most important commissions presented here were recently completed, are under construction, or are still on the drawing boards. There has been little time for clients and building users to assess Johnson's buildings, for critics to reflect on the work, or even for the architect himself to stand back and take stock. Moreover, although he readily describes the functional characteristics of his buildings, Johnson has been, to date, rarely willing to speculate on his emotional wellsprings. Fixing an image of his present practice is like trying to capture the flight of a rapidly moving projectile.

Compounding this problem is the fact that Johnson's work has been so fluid. His extraordinary ability to synthesize ideas quickly has helped to produce an oeuvre that seems, on casual inspection, to lack unity. Although obvious affinities link several of the projects—the schools in New Mexico of the mid-1980s, for example, or the schools in Troy, Michigan, and Perry, Ohio of the early 1990s—the work as a whole ranges dramatically in scale and appearance. What unites the small, profoundly earthbound Desert View Elementary School in Sunland Park, New Mexico with the soaring ticketing hall at O'Hare airport? How is it that the same architect, in less than ten years, could envision the Gothic-style crenellations atop the Tarry Research and Education Building at Northwestern University in Chicago and the sleek curtain walls of the Morton International Building less than two miles away? What can explain the contrast between the cross-axial symmetries of Warsaw Community High School in Indiana, as intricate as any Beaux-Arts competition project, and the dynamic curves and asymmetrical blocks of Temple Hoyne Buell Hall at the University of Illinois in Champaign?

Upon close examination, however, it is clear that the surface shifts in Johnson's projects are not as important as the underlying constants. These are most evident as certain motifs in plan, section, and elevation that thread through the projects, continuously transformed. The variety in the appearance of horizontal building bars opposed against the curving lines of landscape features, for example, or perpendicular spur walls marking the transition between building elements, or walls extruded into towers to mark entrances, starts to suggest the way in which Johnson never discards elements, but constantly transforms them. The kinds of analysis familiar from the modernist versus postmodern stylistic debates of the past two decades do not help much in understanding these shifts. With Johnson's work a given motif, whether traditional or modernist, can appear in a building whose plans and elevations recall the Beaux-Arts masters or the European avant-garde of the early twentieth century. In fact, Johnson has abandoned the struggle between classicism and modernism in favor of an architecture that explores their common bases. It is not by chance that a number of Johnson's favorite architects, notably Eliel Saarinen and Dudok, came of age when it seemed for a moment that these two ways of thinking were not incompatible.

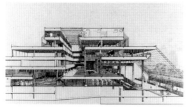

The projects also inspire certain similar feelings. Buildings by Johnson manage to reconcile many contradictory demands placed on them. They merge the personal and intuitive with the systematic and public. A Johnson school always looks reassuringly like a school, an office building like an office building. After spending even a few minutes in any of these buildings most visitors will quickly grasp the underlying spatial order. Virtually without exception the projects featured here are novel and familiar at the same time. Although obviously new, they never strain for innovation or insist on their status as Architecture. These buildings are strong statements, yet defer to their contexts. They represent a desire to embrace and simultaneously reorder diverse environments, to make them more cohesive. Johnson does not issue theoretical or political manifestos nor is he a political activist, yet his work clearly suggests a well-developed sense of social and political purpose.

Training and Early Career: 1948–1976

Ralph Johnson was born in Chicago in 1948 and grew up in the Mount Greenwood neighborhood on the far southwest side of the city. Prior to college his sole exposure to the world of sophisticated, high-art architecture was the discovery of a Frank Lloyd Wright building, the Evans House of 1908, in the adjoining neighborhood of Beverly. (1) By the end of high school, having excelled at mechanical drawing and demonstrated an aptitude for visual thinking, he had decided to become an architect.

Upon entering the University of Illinois at Urbana-Champaign, Johnson was exposed for the first time both to the systematic theories of the Beaux-Arts tradition and to currents in contemporary architecture and art. The most galvanizing of the latter was Paul Rudolph's Christian Science Center (1963) at the university. (2) The Christian Science Center was a potent synthesis of Frank Lloyd Wright's horizontal layering and Le Corbusier's dynamic vertical spatial sequences, and to Johnson it was by far the most interesting building in town. Johnson also broadened his horizons during his undergraduate years by traveling to France, Spain, and Morocco. (5, 6, 7) For his thesis project at Urbana Johnson chose to design a school, using a program that had been written for the institution that eventually became the Olive Harvey Community College on Chicago's South Side. This early design reveals certain characteristic motifs that would have a remarkable persistence in his later work; for example, the relationship of the building's extruded horizontal mass to the discreet spaces appended for special purposes. (3, 4)

After graduating in 1971 Johnson accepted a job in the office of Stanley Tigerman in Chicago. Here he learned about the work of John Hejduk and young architects and artists who were not yet well known, and about Tigerman's own projects; for example, the Miesian grids of the Boardwalk Apartments, on which Johnson worked, and the pinwheeling forms of St. Benedict's Abbey Church in Benet Lake, Wisconsin (1969–73). (8) After his short stint in Tigerman's office, Johnson went on to complete his graduate degree at the Harvard University Graduate School of Design in 1973 and to work in a number of small firms in Florida and Ohio. His first completed building, Astronaut Hall Observatory and Classroom Building in Cocoa, Florida (1973–75), was a neat exercise in the modernist modes of the late 1960s and early 1970s. (9) During these years Johnson also started to enter and win design competitions. His scheme for apartment buildings on Roosevelt Island in New York included intricately layered apartment units that recalled the work of Josep Lluis Sert and Paul Rudolph, and it won an honorable mention in 1975. His housing scheme for Biscayne West won first place in an ideas competition for Miami and was exhibited at the University of Miami in 1976. He also started work on a highly ambitious competition entry for the Pahlavi National Library in Teheran, Iran.

Early Years at Perkins & Will: 1976–1980

When Johnson applied for a job with Perkins & Will in 1976, the firm was one of the largest architectural offices in Chicago and enjoyed a solid reputation for producing hospitals and other complicated buildings. Perkins & Will was originally founded by Lawrence B. Perkins and Philip Will, Jr. in 1935. Perkins was the son of the well-known Prairie School architect Dwight Perkins, so it is not surprising that the firm's early residential commissions were usually low, horizontal buildings with protective overhanging roofs, although they probably owed more to the residential work of Frank Lloyd Wright than to the school buildings on which Dwight Perkins had made his reputation. The firm's big break came in 1938 when it was selected as associate architect for Eliel and Eero Saarinen on the famous Crow Island School in Winnetka, Illinois. (10, 11) This school, with its low, informal classrooms, each equipped with large windows looking out to small gardens and the surrounding landscape, became almost overnight a landmark in American school design. Over the next several decades features of this school were adapted hundreds of times in schools throughout the country, many designed by Perkins & Will. In the best of these, such as Heathcote Elementary School in Scarsdale, New York, of 1953, the balance between sheltered privacy and intimate connection with the landscape made the buildings ideal environments for a new postwar curriculum that stressed individual discovery over rote learning.

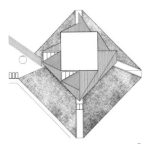

9

10

By the late 1950s the firm's growing volume of school work had been supplemented by other kinds of commissions, notably health care facilities, which soon generated a large percentage of the firm's revenue. Perkins & Will's stylistic vocabulary was diverse. In some commissions, like the 1953 headquarters and research laboratories for the International Minerals and Chemical Corporation in Skokie, Illinois, simple volumes and thin curtain walls reflected the growing influence of Mies van der Rohe. A more decorative or monumental use of modern elements prevailed in other structures, such as the United States Gypsum Building in Chicago, of 1963. Elsewhere a return to features used in the Prairie School was evident in buildings designed in the 1960s and 1970s, for example, Rockford College in Illinois.

Virtually all of these commissions were good examples of their type, but few created any major stir in the design community. Perkins & Will was widely considered somewhat weak in design direction, and there was a considerable feeling within the firm that something should be done. This was exactly the kind of opportunity Johnson welcomed. He threw himself into his work, participating on a number of projects, notably a large hospital at Wafa Wa Amal in Egypt, under the direction of more senior architects in the office. His own first major project was a pavilion for psychiatric and alcoholism treatment programs at Ingalls Memorial Hospital in Harvey, Illinois. Working with August Battaglia, who entered the Perkins & Will office in 1978 and quickly became Johnson's right-hand man, Johnson produced an ingenious scheme whose internal courtyards and streets provided a novel and highly effective therapeutic environment. The building, completed in 1982, was greeted with enthusiasm by the clients, published with approving commentary in *Architectural Record*, and included at the juried Chicago Architecture Club exhibit at the Art Institute of Chicago. It appeared to be the breakthrough Johnson needed in his search for larger, more conspicuous commissions. Unfortunately, the success at Ingalls hospital was undermined by a disappointing experience with a large addition at the University of Chicago Medical Center. Assigned the project, Johnson felt that, given the context of that university's long-standing tradition of Gothic-style masonry structures, the building should have facades of limestone and fairly specific references to the surrounding buildings. The clients felt otherwise, and the building was completed by other designers at Perkins & Will.

11

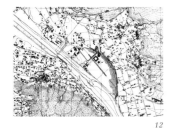

The Encounter with European Rationalism: 1980–1983

At this critical moment in his career Johnson was awarded a Plym Traveling Fellowship from his alma mater, the University of Illinois, and traveled in Europe for six months in 1980. The Plym travel year was a defining event for Johnson; it went far toward helping him resolve one of the most difficult issues in the University of Chicago commission: respecting context. In the United States this issue had become the touchstone for the architects commonly known as postmodernists. Lambasting what they considered the ahistorical, abstract forms of the modernists, they advocated plans and elevations that borrowed from the existing architectural context.

This current made Johnson uneasy. Although he had no moral problems with incorporating design elements from earlier periods, the arbitrariness of unsystematic borrowing and anything resembling pastiche bothered him. With the cacophony of built form in the American city, moreover, what buildings should constitute the essential context? A group of European architects known as the rationalists, or the Tendenza, offered a more appealing alternative. The group, including Aldo Rossi and other architects based primarily in Italy, Switzerland, and southern Europe, believed that familiar urban architectural elements like galleries and arcades and axial, symmetrical compositional schemes had been in use for so long in European cities that they had entered the "collective subconscious." Using these elements but stripping them of any specific stylistic dress that might appeal to nostalgia, many rationalists believed they could create an architecture that was genuinely popular and easily legible but resistant to what they considered the literal copying of the postmodernists.

The Plym fellowship allowed Johnson to visit a number of buildings in Italy. He noted, for example, the almost haunting clarity of Aldo Rossi's school in Fagnano Olona, outside Milan (1978), but what most caught his eye were buildings in the Ticino area of Switzerland, notably a school in Losone by Livio Vacchini and Aurelio Galfetti (1973–75), with an elaborate Palladian plan and a facade that was quite Miesian. (12, 13) The idea that clear, simple public architecture could use traditional plans without necessarily relying on traditional elevations was liberating. Another influential design was a public swimming complex in Bellinzona by Galfetti, in association with Flora Ruchat and Ivo Trümpy (1967–70). Its elements were strung along a central spine that stretched across a highway, reconnecting two parts of the town split by it. (14) For Johnson this kind of design promised a discipline and order that neither abstract modernism nor literal historical borrowing could offer.

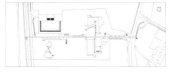

Johnson returned to Perkins & Will and found himself back in the position he had occupied at the outset of his career in that office. Most of the solid commissions went to other designers. He received a quirky set of projects with very uncertain prospects for completion, but these projects allowed him to explore the ideas he had absorbed in Europe.

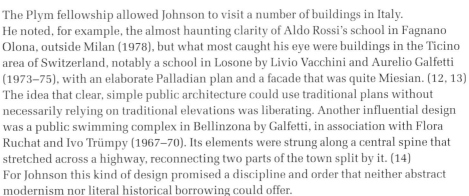

15

16

Johnson's designs for the Solar-Ray building, an office and headquarters in Peoria, Illinois, and the Ocean Club, a large hotel in Miami Beach, both called for axial, symmetrical plans. The section and elevation drawings for Solar-Ray, however, showed a thoroughly modern steel and glass structure that incorporated advanced solar energy technologies. The Ocean Club's terraces and curvilinear pools simultaneously evoked Miami's art deco hotels of the 1930s and Morris Lapidus's work from the 1950s. (15) In his design for a third unbuilt project, the Music Center at Pacific Lutheran University in Tacoma, Washington, Johnson assembled a set of elements greatly favored by the rationalists, including a lobby rotunda, an open covered walkway that helped circulation between several different levels of the campus, a long bar of practice rooms, and a pavilion that served as the concert hall. To unite these elements on the steep site, Johnson used a shifted grid that related to the layout of the campus on the one hand and to the contours of the land and the view toward Mt. Rainier on the other. This device had appeared in the work of Richard Meier and other American architects of the day, but probably came to Johnson's attention through Colin Rowe's writings on urban planning and through the work of the architects in Ticino. Although none of the three projects was ultimately built, the beautifully rendered perspectives were widely published and generated a good deal of favorable publicity—particularly for the Music Center, which won a *Progressive Architecture* design award in 1984. Because *Progressive Architecture* tended to favor young architects and small, personal projects that showed a high degree of novelty and promise, the award was considered a coup for a designer in a large commercial office. Johnson had clearly re-entered the category of promising young architect.

Three Schools: 1984–1987

Johnson further explored the lessons learned in Europe in a set of three school commissions built in the mid-1980s in New Mexico and Indiana. Johnson had long been attracted to the school as a building type because it was an important public building with a manageable scale and contained a variety of spaces, permitting an interesting plan. Soon after he started work at Perkins & Will, moreover, he began to absorb a kind of firm mystique about educational buildings. He had heard about Crow Island School even before joining the office, and at Perkins & Will he worked frequently with William Brubaker, a senior statesman at the firm, a widely known figure in educational circles, and the main client contact for many of the firm's school commissions.

By curious coincidence, about the time the three schools were under construction Johnson found a copy of a book on the schools designed by Dwight Perkins. The typically symmetrical compositions included axial pathways alternating with rectangular courtyards formed by a gymnasium on one side, an auditorium on the other, and a bar of classrooms in between. (16) The discovery reinforced Johnson's belief that certain simple, easily read configurations transcend stylistic periods. About this time he also became acquainted with another rationalist project, the extremely influential scheme

17

18

by Leon Krier for a school in St. Quentin-en-Yvelines, France (1978). Krier separated the elements of this school into individual form types and combined them in a strongly axial arrangement to create a kind of academic village.(17)

In a similar manner, for Capital High School in Santa Fe, Johnson started with the main programmatic elements grouped into axial, symmetrical patterns. He then had to accommodate this ideal scheme to a sharp drop in elevation on one side of the site and the pragmatic need to provide separate entrances for students and the community. The result was a set of two primary progressions of axial spaces at a slight angle to each other and connected by a series of hinge elements. This relatively simple solution solved the knotty problem of keeping functions as close together as possible for ease of access while separating their entrances to avoid mutual interference. The imagery of Capital High School derives from public buildings in the area dating from the territorial era, prior to New Mexico's statehood. At first glance it might seem that here Johnson veered perilously close to the literal pastiche of the postmodernists. Certainly the materials, scale, and details of the buildings quite forcefully recall earlier Santa Fe structures, but the historical elements are so transformed that many visitors are reminded of quite different public buildings; for example, the stripped classical American work of the 1930s. The result is a complex, resonant imagery.

At Desert View Elementary School in Sunland Park, Johnson turned for inspiration to the surrounding agricultural buildings because there was almost no tradition of major public buildings in this rural and relatively poor corner of the state. In this project, how-ever, the sources were so abstracted and transformed through the use of new materials and colors that their specific agricultural imagery became only a faint echo. Indeed, the contrast between the rubble stone walls and the brightly painted metal roof trusses of the three nearly identical structures evokes at once a welcoming domestic feeling and a monumentality that is appropriate for public buildings serving as the major structures in their respective subdivisions.

Again at Warsaw Community High School in Warsaw, Indiana, the surrounding area had no indigenous public building tradition. Johnson chose to model his building on the agricultural structures found in the vicinity, especially the large barns and grain elevators. The result was a set of barnlike structures clad in vertical metal siding with standing seam metal roofs. (18) In the original scheme they would have appeared to form a small village much like the one proposed by Leon Krier. Although a number of elements were dropped for budgetary reasons, compromising the scheme in section, the entire complex is still admirably clear and compact in its planning and the elevations ingenious in their adaptation of agricultural imagery. Still, it is hard to avoid feeling that the fairly literal evocation of regional agricultural buildings is problematic. Understandably, Johnson did not think that what served as the school in many Midwestern towns—a standard-issue brick box with classical trim—was appropriate for a contemporary school with a vastly expanded program at the town's periphery. But was agricultural imagery the right solution? Although the Warsaw school was surrounded by cornfields, the site was not really rural in character but suburban. All three school buildings were well received and widely published, bu the problem of context still loomed large in Johnson's mind.

Orland Park and Morton International Building,
An Expanded Vocabulary: 1987–1990

Even before the schools were completed, Johnson was already exploring the problem of context from a somewhat different angle in a pair of larger, more conspicuous commissions erected almost simultaneously between 1987 and 1990. Both Orland Park Village Center in suburban Chicago and the Morton International Building near the heart of downtown Chicago clearly belong to the sequence of buildings that began with the schools, but an exploration of new ideas and new formal elements led to the creation of buildings quite different, at least in their superficial appearance.

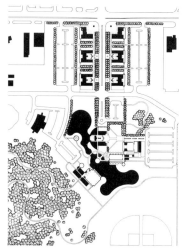

At Orland Park, Johnson's chief problem was to create a forceful civic presence in a small complex that would be dwarfed in scale by the adjacent commercial strip along the village's principal commercial artery—notably the huge regional shopping center that functioned as the de facto village center. To give his buildings the visual impact they deserved, Johnson went beyond the actual commission and fashioned an entire precinct, providing axial approaches from the south and east. (19) At Orland Park the central focus of the composition switches from figural solids—for example, those of the Warsaw Community High School plan—to figural voids, in this case the village green and the amphitheater. From the amphitheater Johnson arranged buildings in radial fashion, overlaying this pattern with a grid responding to the village green. Tying the composition together were circulation paths, located off the main axes of the buildings. The result was an intricate tartan plaid of axes and counter axes. The same kinds of interlocking elements also appear in the elevations, where the vertical support elements, horizontal string courses, and roof planes, all picked out in white, are interwoven with the warm red brick of the walls.

The effect, complex and rich, defies an easy stylistic label. Most of the individual elements, including the arcades and pavilions, had appeared in earlier Johnson buildings. But here the rationalists' legacy is enriched with elements Johnson had seen earlier in his career in the buildings of Frank Lloyd Wright and Paul Rudolph. In addition, the influence of Dudok is already clear at Orland Park, although Johnson's first-hand encounter with Dudok's work came only after the project was under construction, when Johnson and Battaglia visited the city of Hilversum, the Netherlands, in January, 1989. As director of public works for Hilversum for several decades starting in 1915,

19

20

21

22

Dudok had been concerned with creating public buildings that would give focus to the somewhat diffuse garden city. In fact, Dudok often presented his work with the same kind of figure-ground drawings that Johnson so admired in the work of the Italian rationalists, and his removal of superfluous detail reflected the influence of the De Stijl movement and Frank Lloyd Wright. (20, 21, 22) It was almost as if Johnson's entire career to date had been preparing him for the trip to Hilversum. In Dudok, Johnson had found a soul mate.

Throughout the late 1980s Johnson turned to Dudok's work for lessons in how to create buildings that are restrained but never dull, inviting but monumental, highly personal but systematic and orderly. The Orland Park buildings exhibit all of these qualities. Together they create a complex that does not attempt to challenge the architecture of the commercial strip but instead exists alongside it, substituting an intense unity for the strip's larger scale and almost riotous diversity. Inside, Johnson's buildings have all the clarity found in early-twentieth-century civic structures. Like these structures, they rely on good proportions rather than expensive detailing, promising a long life and maximum flexibility.

Although at first glance quite different in appearance, the Morton International Building exhibits many of the qualities seen in the suburban civic center. This building is particularly interesting because a slightly earlier Johnson office building nearby, 123 North Wacker Drive, completed in 1986, allows the viewer to gauge the process by which ideas not entirely resolved in one context are then corrected, refined, and elaborated in another. At Wacker Drive, Johnson first faced the challenge of the large speculative office building, a type largely shunned by the rationalists because of its vast scale and the economic imperatives that usually dictate a thin covering of undifferentiated open space. This is hardly a program that encourages buildings sympathetic to the scale and texture of European cities or even prewar American cities. The final, built version of the Wacker Drive building was not entirely satisfying to Johnson. His attempt to merge the solidity of traditional stone cladding with the lightness of more recent curtain walls was not wholly successful. The pyramidal top of the building, although a striking object on the skyline, particularly when lit at night, came just a little too close to the deco-style buildings that were springing up in great numbers in American cities. Nevertheless, the Wacker Drive building had considerable presence from the street, received positive reviews in the architectural press, and led directly to Johnson's selection as one of seven top American designers in *Fortune* magazine. To many potential business clients of a large commercial firm like Perkins & Will, this was the ultimate accolade. In turn, it gave Johnson a considerably more powerful voice at the firm.

23

At the Morton International Building both the complicated site, located in part over active rail lines, and the complex program provided Johnson with the stimulus to create a richer building, one wedded more specifically to its site yet without obviously copied stylistic elements. The program, which required a bulky base and slim office floor plates, justified a forthrightly asymmetrical structure, something Johnson had been eager to explore after the elaborate symmetries of the schools. He found an excellent example in the low podium and vertical tower of George Howe and William Lescaze's famous Philadelphia Saving Fund Society Building, designed in the late 1920s and completed in 1931. (23) The Philadelphia building, conceived at a time when European modern ideas were first making their way into mainstream American practice, provided Johnson with ideas about how to create a facade that had weight and solidity but also large transparent areas. The Morton International Building is so successful in reconciling the seemingly contradictory needs of site and program that most viewers are completely unaware of its great variety of facade materials and fenestration treatments. Nor are they aware of the difficulty the architect faced in shoehorning public spaces into a site where much of the lower-level square footage was usurped by railroad tracks, parking ramps, and service entrances. Johnson turned this problem into a virtue. The major public spaces, including the lobby, the riverfront esplanade, and the walkway along the river, seem energized by compression rather than cramped by the inadequate space.

Perry Community Education Village and International Terminal,
O'Hare International Airport: 1989–1995

By 1990 Ralph Johnson's career had definitively taken off. At Perkins & Will, it was Johnson who won most of the awards and who was most responsible for changing the firm's reputation from that of a large, technically competent organization to an innovative design office. This combination proved highly effective. During the boom years of the late 1980s and early 1990s, Perkins & Will surged ahead of Chicago's long-time leading architectural offices in the dollar value of new commissions. Among Johnson's new commissions was a pair of school complexes: one in Troy, Michigan, and the other in Perry, a small but rapidly growing northeast Ohio community.

At Perry the work encompassed what was to become an entire educational village. Although the elementary and middle schools are still under construction, the completed high school affords an opportunity to study Johnson's most complex and highly elaborate school project to date. Here Johnson largely abandoned his attachment to Beaux-Arts configurations in favor of a scheme in which asymmetrical blocks line up as parallel bars, with various elements pinwheeling from them to create internal courtyards. The result in some ways echoes the earliest Johnson school plans, with their straightforward modernist configurations, notably one at Woodbridge Middle School in Irvine, California. But at Perry the discreet, modernist elements of the earlier school are fused into a much more complex system in which the long classroom bars, the entry towers, and the large-span halls of the assembly and athletic spaces interlock in a tightly ordered pattern of solids and voids and respond to the undulating margin of trees around the site. In elevation, likewise, old archetypal forms favored by the rationalists almost disappear in favor of more modern elements drawn freely from American industrial architecture, the late works of Dudok, and the public buildings of Alvar Aalto. The result is as richly modulated as any Beaux-Arts scheme, but without the classical formal vocabulary.

The Perry school contains some of Johnson's most notable interiors. The administration wing lobby, for example, is chameleon-like. To most visiting parents it probably seems light, airy, and spatially intriguing; but to a student sent there to wait, it almost certainly appears appropriately portentous, like the space outside the principal's office in thousands of American schools. In part this familiar quality derives from the standard-ized, relatively inexpensive materials. The floor is made of a standard sheet material, the walls of brick. But the floor material is cut and inlaid to suggest the circulation pattern of the school and looks like expensive terrazzo. The brick is laid in black courses at the base, topped by buff brick interrupted at regular intervals by a recessed course in a deeper shade. Both treatments give the building a visual ambivalence so often seen in Johnson's projects. Do these walls remind us of a standard American high school constructed around 1915 or a European modernist building of the mid-1930s? As usual, it is both and neither.

24

One of the greatest potential pitfalls in the career of any successful designer is the moment of transition from small commissions to work that is large scale, public, and highly conspicuous. Even for Johnson, who had designed numerous public structures and a handful of large office buildings, the commission for the International Terminal at Chicago's O'Hare airport must have been daunting. No building type in the American city is more complex, more constrained by space limitations, and subject to more program changes than a major airport terminal. None receives more scrutiny from specialists and the general public or is as likely to generate unflattering newspaper headlines when something invariably goes wrong.

25

Despite these problems and exterior pressures, Johnson succeeded in creating one of the most memorable airport terminals of recent years. Because the building is located along the O'Hare access road, which enters the airport at an angle, Johnson started with a group of asymmetrical schemes. (24, 25) In the end, however, the need for a single security checkpoint led to a symmetrical bow-shaped configuration. From land-side, departing passengers cross over the tracks of the people mover to arrive at the ticketing hall. This space, the largest in the composition, vaguely recalls bridges and other infrastructure around the airport, the roofs of large clear-span industrial spaces, and the great train stations of the late nineteenth and early twentieth century. But the careful joinery of the structural members clearly distinguishes it from industrial buildings, and the overwhelming impact of glass and white surfaces distances it from the great halls of travel.

It is also reminiscent of the magnificent but quite different spaces of Helmut Jahn's concourses at O'Hare's United Terminal (1988), a building Johnson greatly admires. The arching roof of Johnson's ticketing hall echoes all of these earlier structures as well as the profile of any number of roofs in earlier Ralph Johnson buildings and the curve in plan at the concourse of the International Terminal itself.

All these elements have been thoroughly assimilated and highly abstracted; for Johnson this process of abstraction defines successful contextualism. The result is a set of luminous interior spaces and a light, soaring image that serves as a gateway for travelers descending into O'Hare in airplanes or arriving in cars along the expressway. Even with the shrinking necessary to fit the entire program into the available footprint and some insensitive modifications made after the building was finished, the lower-level customs area with natural light flooding down from above, the great ticketing hall, and the glassy stations for the people mover are brilliant spatial inventions. It may even be that the spatial compression, while sometimes unfortunate for passengers during the busiest hours, has heightened the drama. The diagonal view from the ticketing hall level down the escalators, through the glass walls of the people mover station toward the incoming passenger areas, takes in one of the most dramatic spaces in contemporary architecture—unexpectedly vertical, high and narrow, light-filled, and optimistically buoyant. Even the most bewildered passengers, disembarking after ten or more hours of flight, can hardly help but marvel at the structure's crystalline precision.

Current Work: 1991-1994

Recent commissions further suggest that Johnson does not settle easily into well-worn paths. In The Woodlands High School in Texas or the laboratories for the Dongbu Corporation in Korea, for example, the parallel or quadrangular bars of earlier buildings have been fashioned into circles or pieces of circles, as though the modernist parallel bars of the schools in Perry and Troy have returned, transformed, to the realm of the Beaux-Arts. The curvilinear forms that usually appear as landscape elements in earlier buildings have been transmuted into built form. At the same time, Johnson's experience working with landscape architect Dan Kiley on the office building at 100 North Wacker Drive in Chicago has strengthened his already considerable appreciation of the interaction between building and land. In the high school for Chelsea, Massachusetts, on the other hand, Johnson has refashioned the forms he created for schools at the urban periphery to fit a dense city fabric, producing a tension between the low horizontal elements seen in many of his early works and the vertical forms necessary for the site.

Among the buildings under construction, perhaps the most challenging for Johnson has been Temple Hoyne Buell Hall at the University of Illinois in Champaign. Schools of architecture have proven notoriously risky commissions for even the most established designers. No building type today receives closer scrutiny from architectural professionals, many of whom seem to specialize in sublimating their untapped design energies into critiques of their working environments.

Unlike most previous Johnson buildings, Buell Hall will have to respond to several architecturally ambitious structures in its immediate context. Diagonally to the north, across the campus's east-west military axis, stands the deceptively simple but highly accomplished neo-Georgian brick facade of Charles Platt's Architecture Building of the 1920s. This structure, with its elegant Palladian cadences, defines the southern edge of a quadrangle facing north. To the east, across the main north-south axis, stretches the long, flat plane of Helmut Jahn's Agricultural Engineering Sciences Building. To the west, finally, lies the Education Building by A. Richard Williams, which, unlike any of the other buildings in the area, sits in the center of its site, surrounded by landscape. Altogether it is a set of highly varied structures, each seeming to demand a different response. In Johnson's scheme, not surprisingly, building bars to the north and east define the campus axes, but rather than filling out one or both of the remaining sides of the implied rectangle, Johnson has placed the faculty offices in a boldly curving bar that barely touches the perpendicular blocks at the perimeter of the site before floating free above a stepped courtyard. The high, tightly bounded space defined by these three elements, like a theater lobby with its stairs and balconies, promises to be one of the most interesting Johnson has created.

Although the central space of Buell Hall promises to look quite different from any interior Johnson has created, it will clearly have many affinities with his earlier work. As in the past, the elements probably will be resolved in a way that is as orderly and systematic as the origins of the motifs are apparently circuitous and haphazard. Moreover, Johnson's recent work continues to reveal a constant dialog between the architect and the city, and his effort to at once extend and correct the existing fabric with each new building. Johnson's projects are exercises in balancing invention and vitality with the order necessary to transform urban fabric into neighborhoods, communities, and cities.

Schools INDIVIDUAL & COMMUNITY

Schools should encourage a student's individual learning experience and simultaneously foster a sense of academic community. Schools should also reflect and reinforce the patterns of society. The educational factory of the past is too anonymous to achieve these goals; it must be scaled down into smaller clusters so the school becomes a microcosm of society—a kind of village—and responds to the individual child's needs. By analyzing the building program and translating it into typological elements, the architect can transform a large school into a series of smaller, more comprehensible and accessible social units.

In many American communities the school is beginning to replace the neighborhood and family life as a social structure that provides support to children. Schools can also help to reinforce community structure; but to do so, physical barriers between the institution and the community must be dismantled. In addition, applying tradition and history to the design of schools can produce meaningful symbolic connections to our collective memory and culture. The modern school should respond to both our age of information and the lessons of traditional forms.

The Woodbridge Middle School in Irvine, California, was an early attempt to treat the school as a villagelike cluster of forms. Subsequent schools in Santa Fe and Sunland Park, both in New Mexico, and in Warsaw, Indiana refine this idea. In these schools typological elements connect form and program. Each program element has its own shape and clearly stands apart from its neighbor, yet is tied to the whole by a strongly ordered plan. The later schools for Troy, Michigan; Perry, Ohio; and Singapore explore a similar theme in more freely grouped linear classroom bars and objectlike assembly spaces. With this fragmented massing each building adjusts to local site conditions and the complex as a whole becomes permeable to its natural surroundings. The school for Chelsea, Massachusetts is an application of the village concept in an urban setting. Manipulating the sections and massing achieved a vertically condensed version of the earlier rural schemes.

Desert View Elementary School, Sunland Park, New Mexico 1985–1988

Woodbridge Middle School

Irvine, California 1978–1982

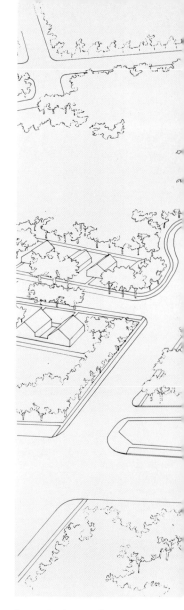

Woodbridge Middle School was designed for a site in a low-density residential area of Irvine, a large planned community south of Los Angeles. The 750-student school consists of a series of permeable interior and exterior spaces; this scheme takes advantage of the mild Southern California climate and provides a seamless connection to the surrounding community park system. Because the school has three concurrent teaching systems and varying enrollments, flexibility was a primary design concern.

The building is organized into two zones, one for teaching and one for shared functions, on either side of an exterior arcaded circulation spine. The teaching zone is housed in a clerestoried loft with movable partitions designed to accommodate fluctuations in the student population. The outdoor circulation spine links the groups of classrooms in the teaching loft to the media center, cafeteria, physical education facilities, and other shared spaces. A multilevel courtyard to the west of this spine is the school's central focal element. The library and other quiet areas are north of this courtyard; the noisier dining and physical education spaces are to the south, adjacent to the playfields. A system of layered walls on the school's perimeter provides a sun screen and allows for larger areas of glass on the exterior of the teaching loft.

Perspective from south

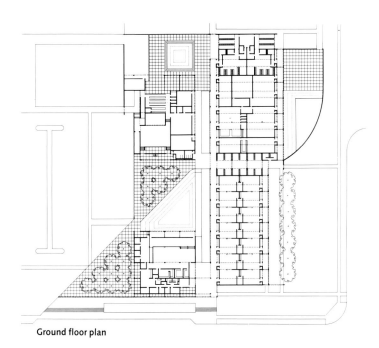

Ground floor plan

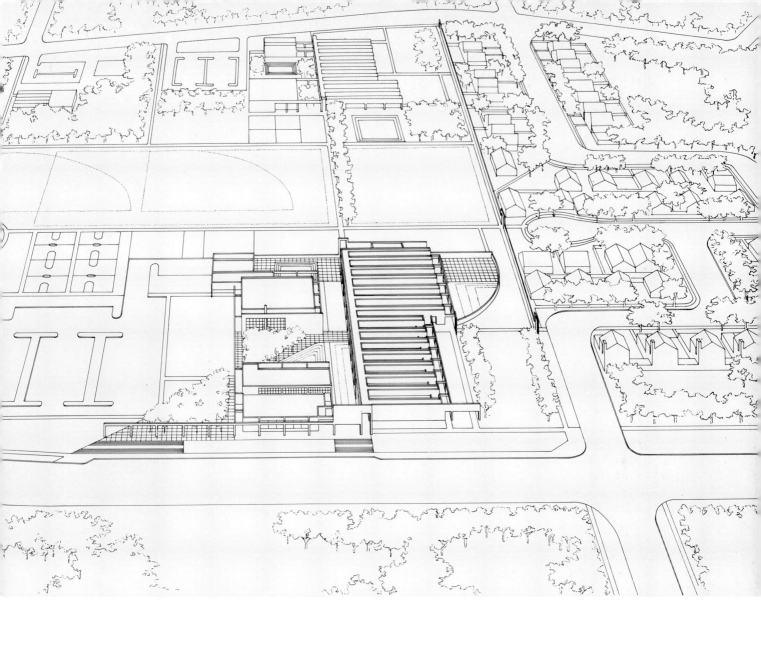

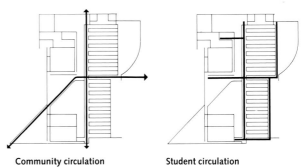

Community circulation   Student circulation

Capital High School

Santa Fe, New Mexico 1984–1988

Capital High School stands on an open plain at the southern edge of Santa Fe. Unlike the historic center of Santa Fe, this area is characterized by residential and commercial suburban sprawl. The school draws upon the architectural traditions of central Santa Fe to counteract this sprawl and to provide a focal structure for the community.

The scheme takes advantage of views and special site conditions, including an arroyo that crosses the northwest portion of the site. Six form types common to Santa Fe's architecture—colonnade, loft, courtyard, hall, pavilion, and tower—house each of the school's functions. Loftlike classroom pavilions and specialized pavilions for drama, dining, and music cluster on an axis oriented toward distant mountains, while the gymnasium and playfields sit on the north-south axis. Towers and arcades unite the pavilions and recall the territorial style typical of Santa Fe's civic architecture in the late nineteenth century, prior to statehood. In response to the harsh desert climate, small glazed openings punctuate massive masonry walls. The built elements form a sequence of plazas and courtyards that echo central Santa Fe's urbanism. A colonnaded plaza adjacent to a circular bus drop-off announces the student entrance, while a public plaza provides community access to the gymnasium and theater when the school is closed.

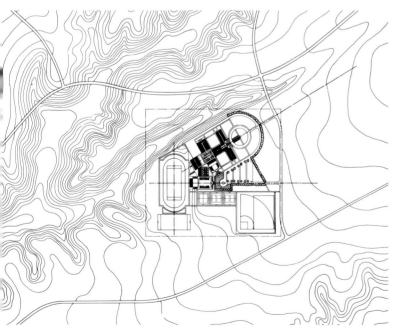

Site plan

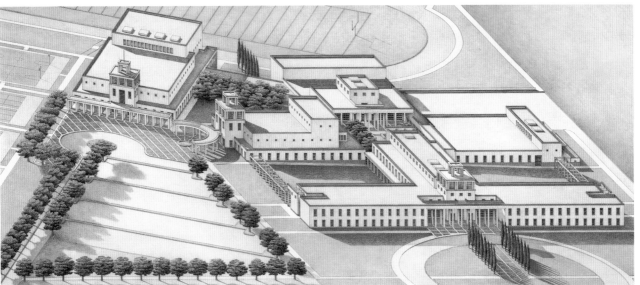

Axonometric

Existing architecture in Sante Fe

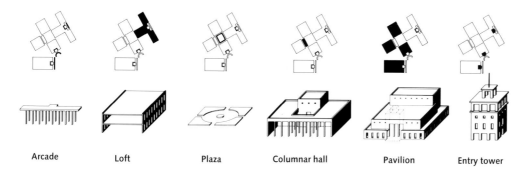

| Arcade | Loft | Plaza | Columnar hall | Pavilion | Entry tower |

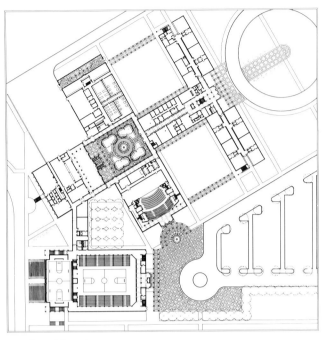

Ground floor plan

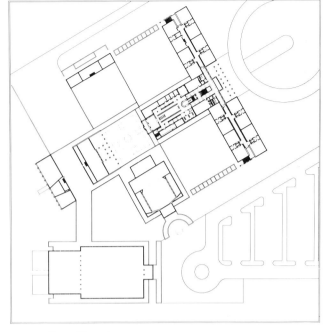

Second floor plan

Desert View Elementary School

Sunland Park, New Mexico 1985–1988

This elementary school for 800 students is one of three schools developed from one prototypical design and built about one-quarter of a mile apart in the arid terrain of southeastern New Mexico. The three sites lie between a fragmented residential area and a railroad line that marks the border with Mexico. On an urban level the project's strong hierarchical form creates a community focal point and brings a sense of cohesion to the residential area. On an educational level the school provides a village-like environment for teaching small children. A low wall of native stone separates the surrounding windswept sand desert from the irrigated planting areas and a cluster of classrooms and shared spaces arranged around variable-sized open courtyards.

A series of formal building types organizes the school's functions. Sheds enclose the repetitive classroom units; larger-scale pavilions house the dining and multipurpose room; punched parallel walls topped by clerestory roofs define major circulation; and translucent fiberglass roofs and canvas awnings define and shade walkways and plazas. These forms were organized hierarchically and axially, with the shared, more public elements at the center of the composition. The forms are monumental in shape but reduced in size, creating the appearance of a small-scale version of a larger building—a building adjusted to a child's size.

The architectural language is an abstraction of the region's residential and agrarian architecture, with masonry bearing walls, exposed steel construction, and sloped metal roofs that recall unassuming and practical detailing.

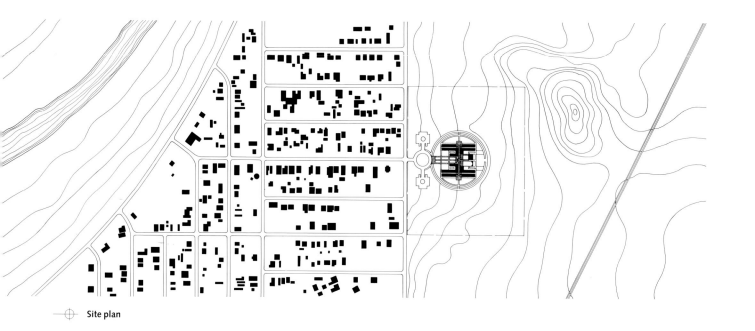

Site plan

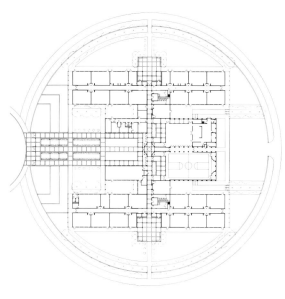

Ground floor plan

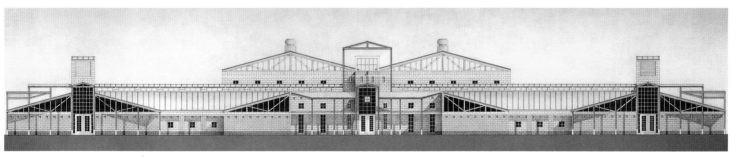

North elevation

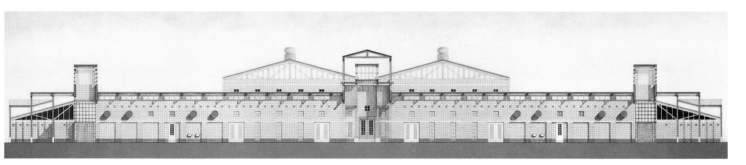

Section

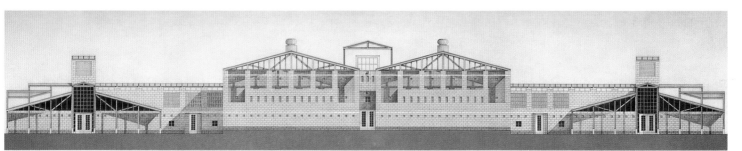

South elevation

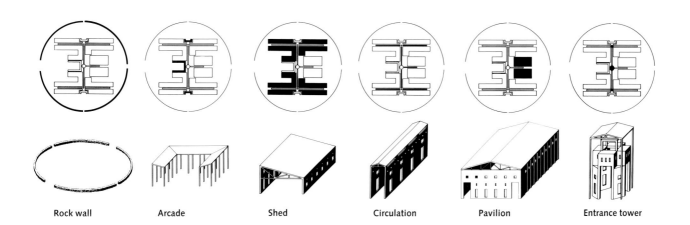

| Rock wall | Arcade | Shed | Circulation | Pavilion | Entrance tower |

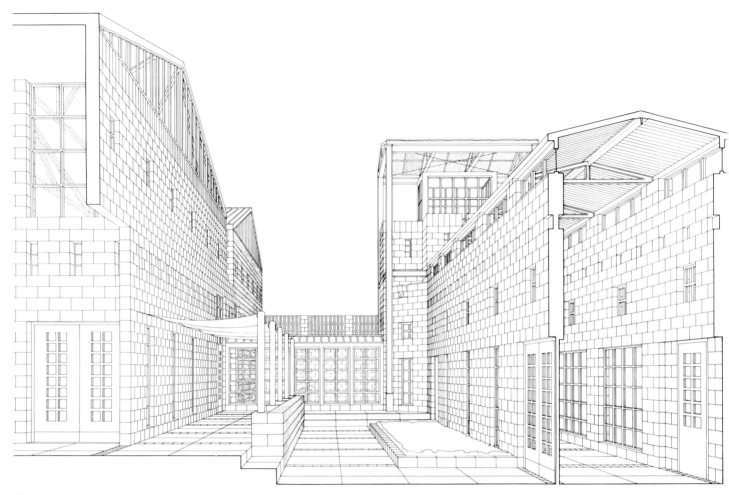

Section perspective at courtyard

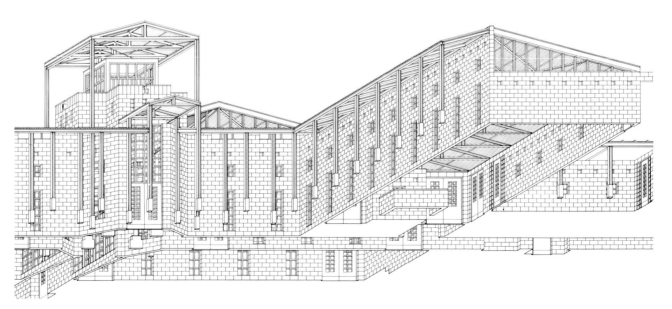

Axonometric entrance

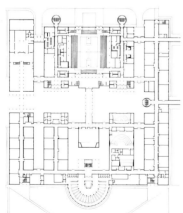

Ground floor plan

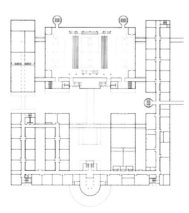

Second floor plan

Warsaw Community High School

Warsaw, Indiana 1987– 1990

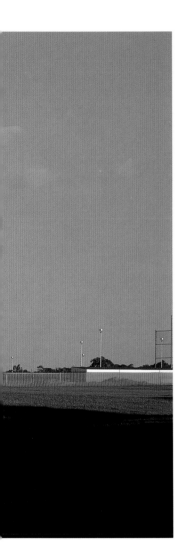

This 2,000-student high school for a town in central Indiana combines agrarian building traditions with the more formal planning concepts of the earlier schools in New Mexico. The relaxed, ad hoc groupings of structures on surrounding farms here assume a more centralized, axial configuration, allowing the school to be read as a public structure.

A circle of trees enclosing the site helps to link the new school to the existing high school building, which is to be renovated as a career center. The trees also delimit the school from the prairie, much the same way as the rock wall mediates between the school and the desert at Desert View Elementary School.

A bar of classrooms forms a wall around three sides of the school and encloses a courtyard whose fourth edge is defined by a large gymnasium. An arched opening in the east wall of the classroom bar allows entry into the central courtyard. This courtyard is an important gathering spot for students during warmer months and provides access to the gymnasium, cafeteria, and meeting room. As the school's central learning resource, the library is the only element allowed to break through the outer edge of the classroom bars.

Site plan

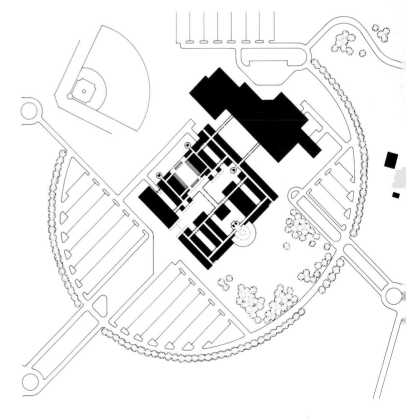

Troy High School

Troy, Michigan 1989–1992

This school for 1,800 students in the expanding Detroit suburb of Troy responds to its site rather than to regional architectural characteristics, weaving together interior and exterior spaces. Similar intentions informed the Crow Island School in Winnetka, Illinois, designed in 1939 by Perkins & Will and Eliel and Eero Saarinen, as well as the nearby Cranbrook Academy of Art in Bloomfield Hills, designed by Eliel Saarinen between 1925 and 1943. But Troy High School also continues the school-as-village theme of earlier projects.

Here parallel classroom bars connected by a central circulation spine sit at right angles to a stand of trees at the southwest corner of the site. The resulting spaces are a series of outdoor rooms that become integral parts of the interior environment of the school. The bars act as a ground or datum that contrasts with the sculptural, pavilion-like forms of the school's shared facilities: the library, cafeteria, auditorium, gymnasium, and pool. The theater and gymnasium are located at the periphery to allow for separate community access. An exit stair transformed into a symbolic tower marks the main entrance and terminates the lobby end of the spine.

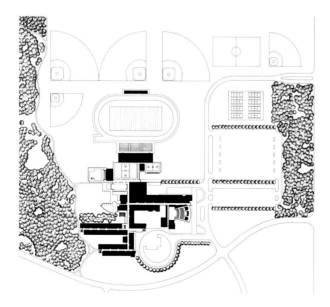

Site plan

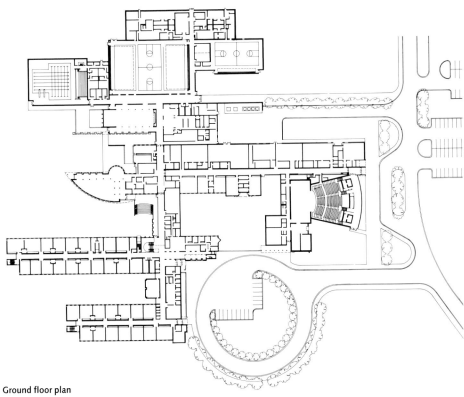

Ground floor plan

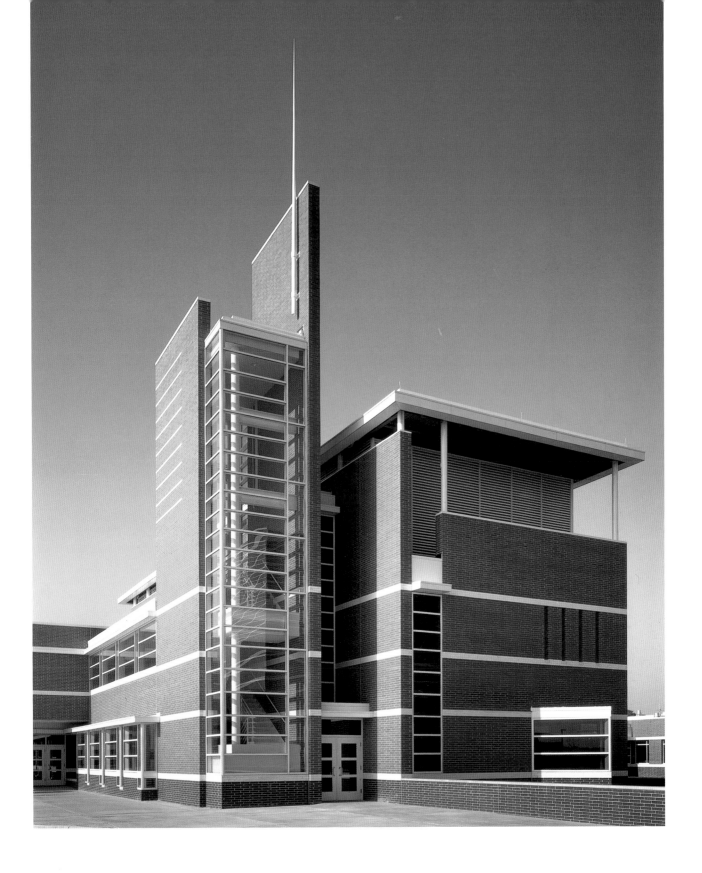

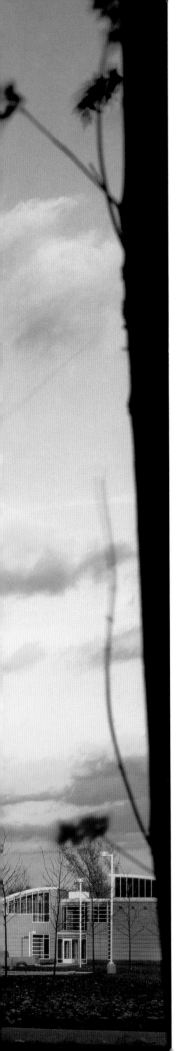

Perry Community Education Village

Perry, Ohio 1990–1995

The design of the Perry school, an educational village for 4,500 students, further explores the organizing principles used in Troy High School. The 160-acre site thirty miles east of Cleveland was once completely forested and has been partially cleared for agricultural use. This campus replaced the school district's aging facilities and consolidated them into a single location.

Mature stands of trees along both banks of a creek divide the site in half. Two separate campuses were created on either side of this creek. The west campus contains the high school and community physical fitness center; the east campus contains the middle and elementary schools. Each campus functions as an individual entity with its own classrooms, laboratories, library, and arts facilities. An enclosed walkway bridges the creek to link all the facilities together. As with Troy High School, the classroom bars form a datum unifying a series of assembly and shared spaces. The project adapts the abstract idea of type to the particularity of the site to organize a complex program into discrete parts. Combining and assembling the parts allows the entire complex to be read as a rich whole. A repetitive, fan-shaped element contains each school's library and music and art department and acts as a mediating device between the school's orthogonal grid and the irregular edge formed by the trees. Towers terminate each end of the connecting walkway and mark the entrance plaza for each campus. A raised press box celebrates the importance of sporting events in the high school student's social life.

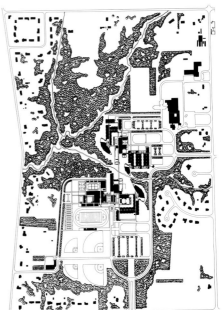

Site plan

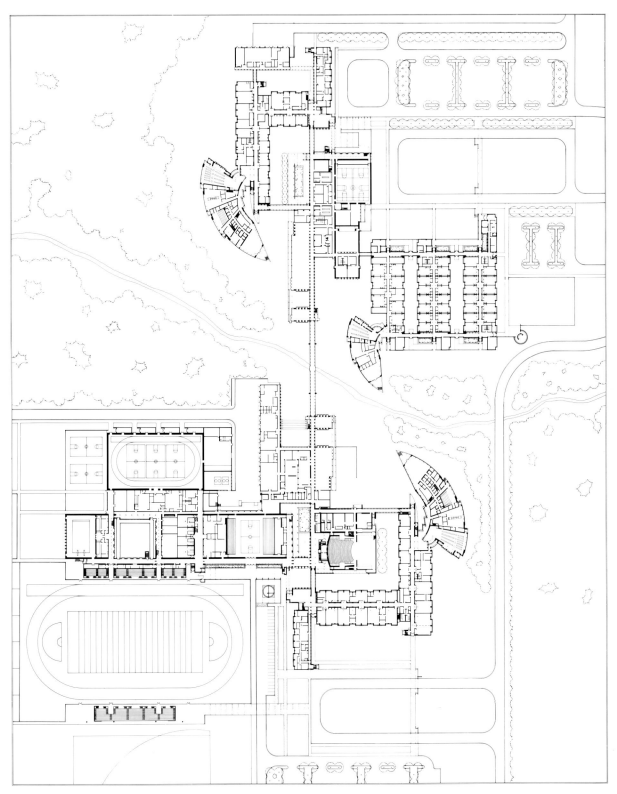

Ground floor plan

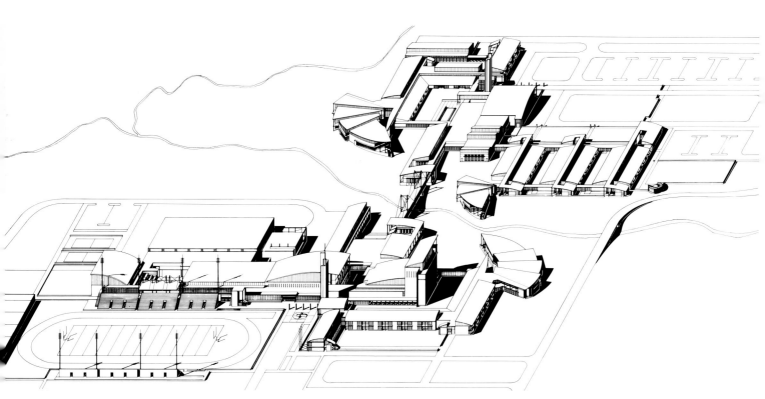

Axonometric

Theater lobby

Press box from north

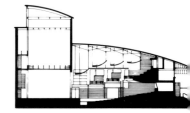

Section

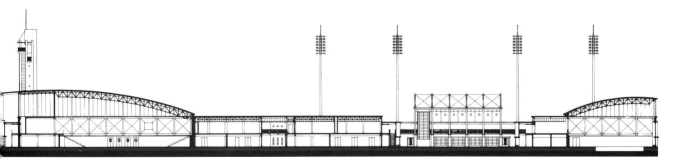

The Woodlands High School

The Woodlands, Texas 1992–1996

In this 3,000-student high school the classrooms form a wall-like enclosure that recalls Warsaw Community High School in Indiana. According to local code all buildings in The Woodlands, a planned community north of Houston, Texas, must be set back behind screens of existing trees. The scheme attempts to create a public architectural setting minimally visible from the street. Carving a large, circular void in this wooded setting created a sense of public identity without the need for a freestanding object.

The circular classroom element overlaps two distinct grids: a community grid aligned with streets adjacent to the property to the north and the grid established by the north-south axis. The spaces shared with the community—the performing arts center, gymnasiums, cafeteria, and library—align with the community grid. The athletic buildings, playfields, and outdoor spaces align

with the cardinal axis to allow for proper solar orientation. Slices through the classroom wall mark where the circle intersects with major sidewalks, entrances, and stairs. The broad overhangs and massive walls with slotlike openings accommodate the harsh Texas sun.

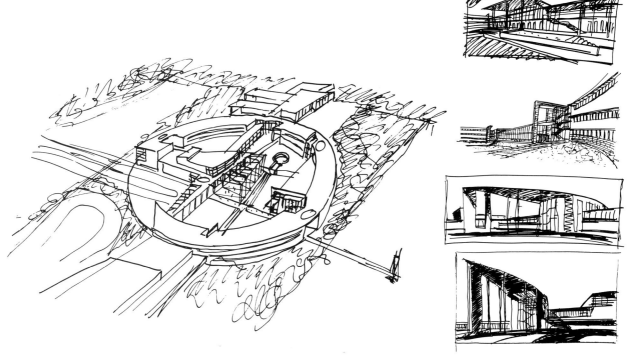

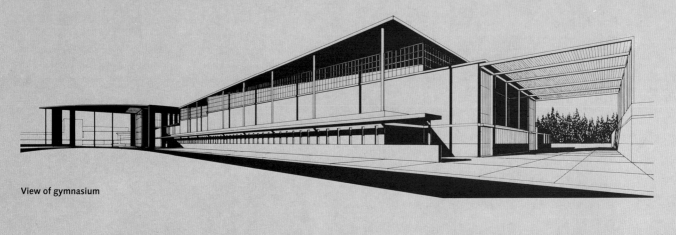

View of gymnasium

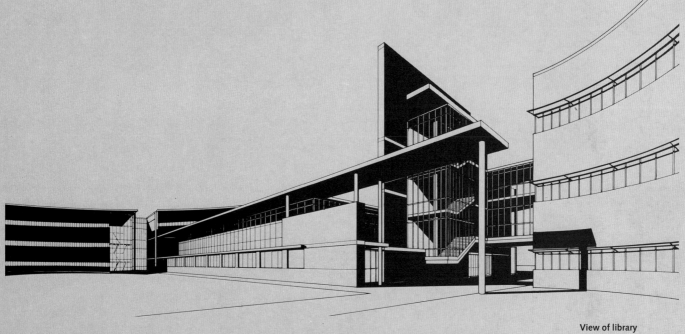

View of library

View of entrance

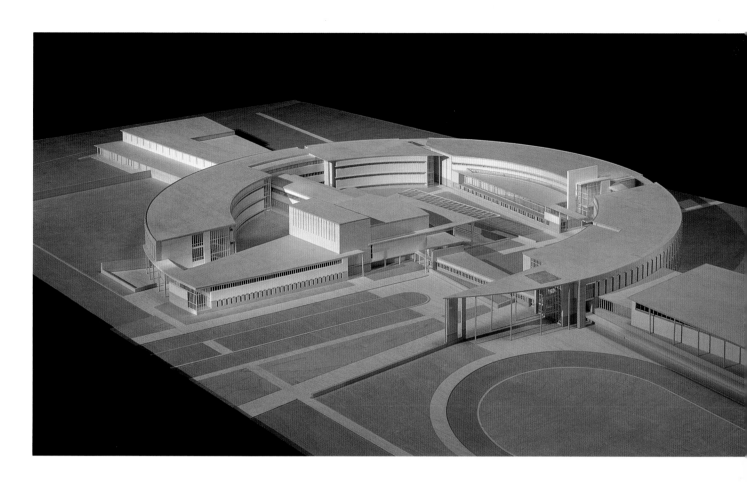

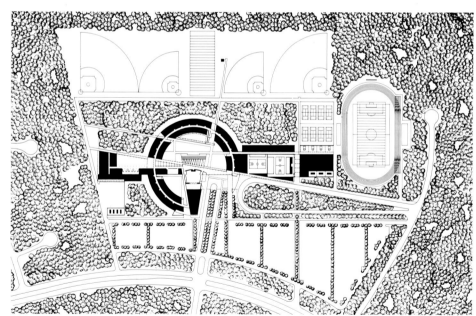

Site plan

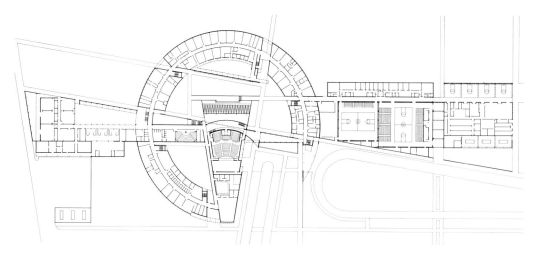

Ground floor plan

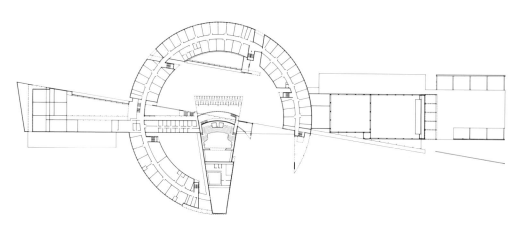

Second floor plan

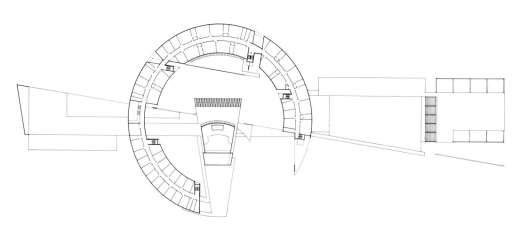

Third floor plan

INDIVIDUAL & COMMUNITY

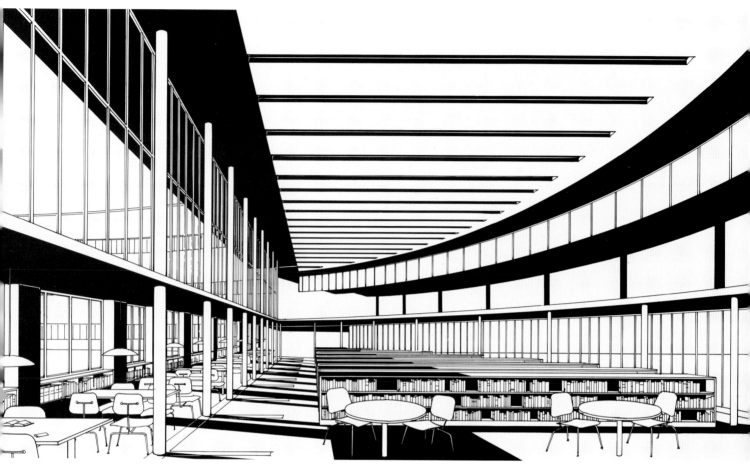

Library

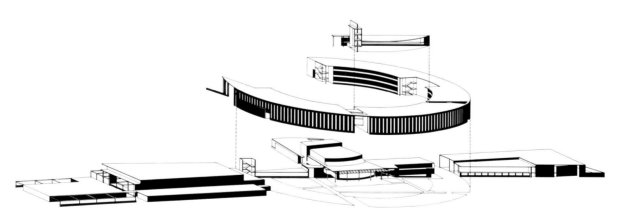

Exploded axonometric

Chelsea High School

Chelsea, Massachusetts 1993–1996

This design for a 1,000-student inner-city high school in the Boston area applies the principles previously explored in rural and suburban schools. Four interdisciplinary and autonomous "houses" provide students with a home base where technological tools support individualized learning. Each house emphasizes instruction in a specific occupation, reinforcing the link between education and employability. Each occupies a separate four-story, rowhouse-like unit with its own staircase and street entrance on the south. These stairs help modulate the south elevation into an expression of the four distinct and autonomous teaching units.

Two community entrances from the east and west lead to a multilevel interior street. This street connects the shared spaces of the school: the auditorium, library, music rooms, and gymnasium to the north, with the four classroom houses and their individual dining spaces to the south. This street is skylit to allow light into the interior classrooms. To the north of the community street an open stair leads to an upper-level clerestoried library that overlooks the playfields to the north and the community street to the south.

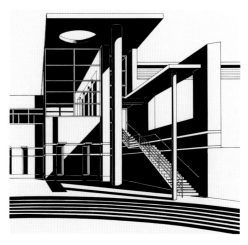

Exterior of library

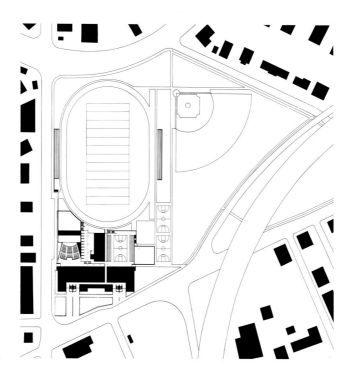

Site plan

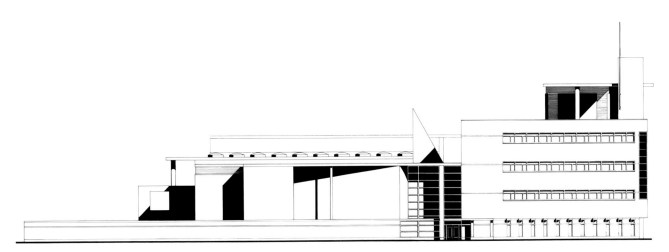

South elevation

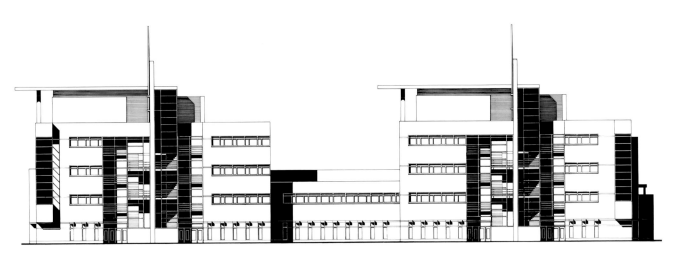

West elevation

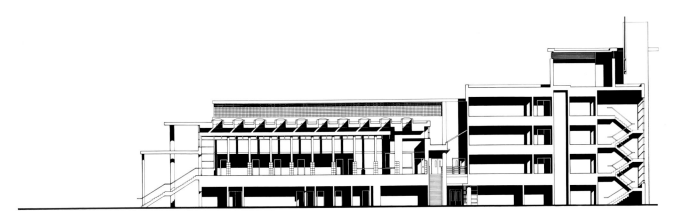

Section

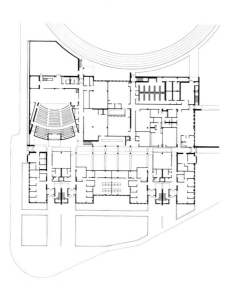

Ground floor plan

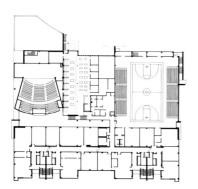

Second floor plan

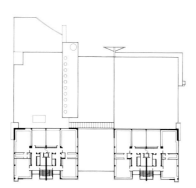

Third floor plan

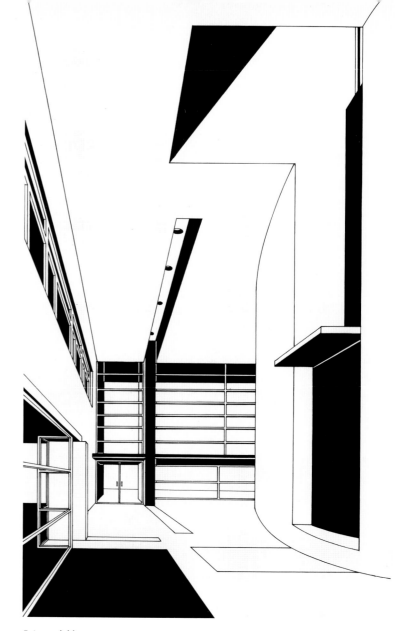

Entrance lobby

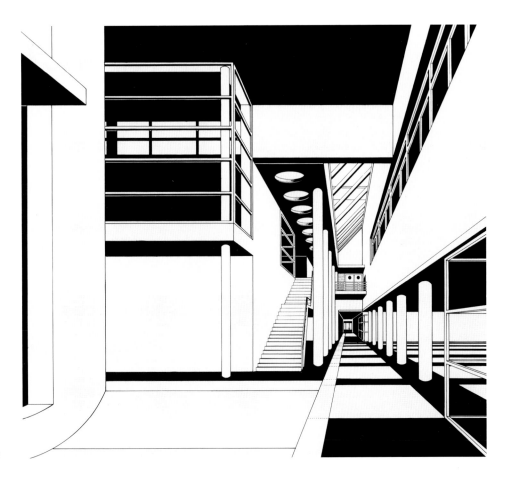

Central corridor

Library

Singapore American School

The Woodlands New Town, Singapore 1993–1996

A new campus for the Singapore American School consolidates two existing schools at a site in The Woodlands, one of the New Towns on the periphery of Singapore near the Malaysian border. The project consists of four self-contained schools for 3,000 students: a pre-school, elementary school, middle school, and high school. The schools share

certain common facilities such as a media center, administrative offices, assembly spaces, and physical education facilities.

Like Capital High School in Santa Fe, this project explores the subtle transformation of regional architecture, in this case the indigenous architecture of Southeast Asia. Large, sloped tile roofs unify the series of parallel classroom bars and shared facilities.

The roof planes provide shade and shed the large volumes of rainwater common in this tropical climate; underneath, shared functions appear as individual objects. Penetrations in the bars at major circulation and entry points provide cross ventilation in the direction of prevailing breezes. The strong horizontal bars with their dominant tile roofs visually organize the various levels of this sloping site.

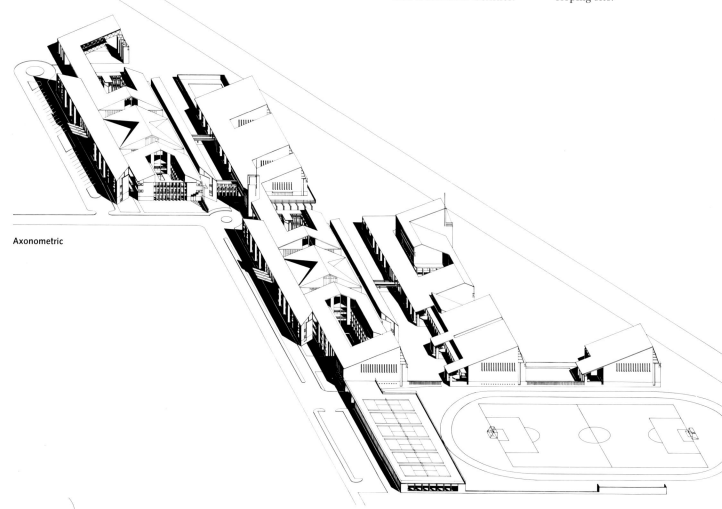

Axonometric

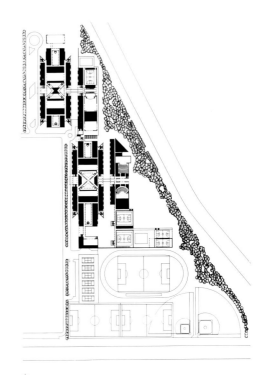

Site plan

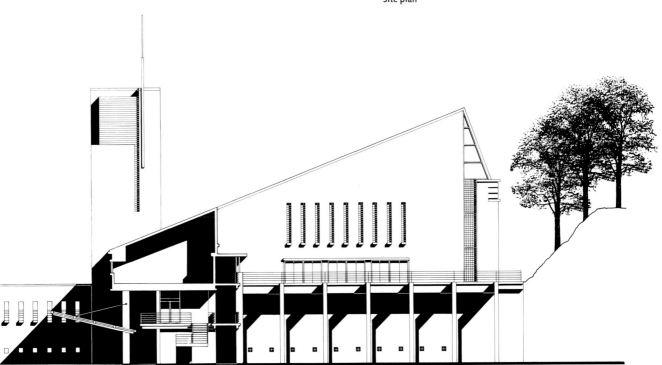

Section-elevation

Buildings for Higher Education CONTINUITY & CIRCUMSTANCE

Most American colleges and universities are based on Thomas Jefferson's precedent, the University of Virginia, where the campus is a self-contained city, an academic village. Initially conceived as clusters of buildings isolated in parklike rural settings, many universities have become landlocked by the cities developing around them. Campuses take on increasingly urban characteristics as new structures are inserted between existing buildings. In addition, the layering of different master plans and architectural styles over the years has produced a rich diversity of built form on many campuses.

Currently much of the new university construction occurs on the campus periphery, which is less defined than the older campus core. Often new sites are available only in areas laid out after World War II, a period when dogmatic modern planning emphasized the individual building over the creation of place. New structures or additions in these areas can act as infill and provide spatial continuity and definition between buildings. The architect should strive to unify and extend existing urban patterns and suggest future directions for growth. To do this requires a thorough understanding of each campus's particular history, traditions, and growth patterns. The campus's plan must be understood as a whole that orders its parts. The form of individual buildings should relate to the needs of site and program, but unplanned or unusual site conditions should be seen as opportunities to create unique places within the overall plan. Specific functional areas such as lobbies or assembly spaces can further heighten this sense of place through their volumetric expression.

In the proposal for a music building at Pacific Lutheran University in Tacoma, Washington, a gateway links the upper and lower campuses, creating new entry spaces and a newly defined campus edge. The Temple Hoyne Buell Hall for the University of Illinois at Urbana-Champaign resolves two major campus axes and defines the edge of existing outdoor public spaces while creating its own private courtyard and interior public spaces. Laboratory additions for the University of Illinois, Northwestern University, and Ohio State University tie together existing structures, provide edge definition, and reinforce circulation patterns. The new campus for Edison Community College represents the effort to establish an urban presence for a developing area west of Naples, Florida.

Tarry Research and Education Building, Northwestern University, Chicago 1986–1990

Music Center

Pacific Lutheran University, Tacoma, Washington 1983

This project was designed to consolidate Pacific Lutheran University's music department into one new facility containing a 600-seat concert hall and a variety of smaller instructional spaces. The site for the Music Center was a wooded slope at the university's western edge, where a 40-foot grade separates the upper and lower campuses. The proposed design connected the upper and lower campuses and created new gateways to both campuses from the west.

Four elemental architectural forms contain the major components of the Music Center and respond to the unique site: a pavilion (concert hall), a rotunda (public lobby), a linear repetitive structure (practice rooms), and an open-air colonnade. These components are aligned along two major axes. The colonnade runs along a line perpendicular to views of Mount Rainier to the east and connects the two campuses. The colonnade frames views of the mountain, forms a visual filter to the complex, and modulates its scale.

The practice rooms, aligned with the north-south orthogonal campus grid, form a strong landscape element terminating the western edge of the campus. The pavilion also aligns with this axis. Locating the rotunda at the intersection of the two axes gives it symbolic importance as the building's major public interior space. Openings in the rotunda also frame views of Mount Rainier.

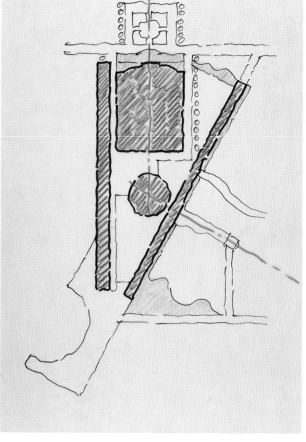

Site plan

Plan sketch

Axonometric

View from campus

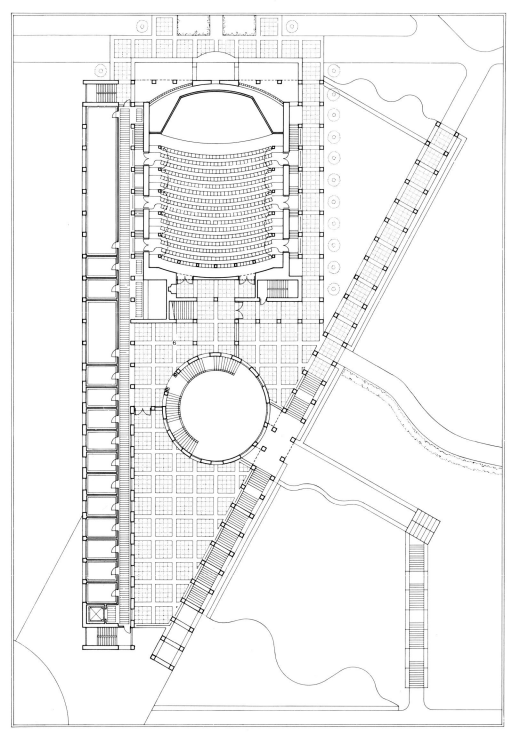

Ground floor plan

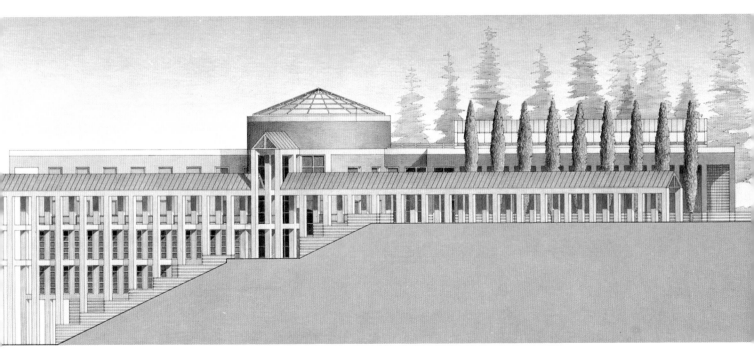

East elevation

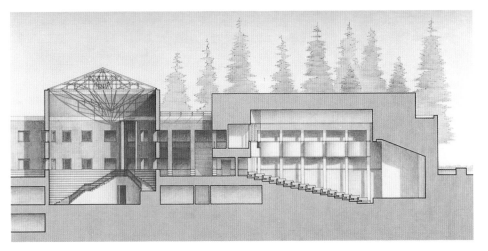

Section

Lobby

Tarry Research and Education Building

Northwestern University, Chicago 1986–1990

Located on a constricted site east of Michigan Avenue on the near north side of Chicago, this fifteen-story research tower provides teaching and laboratory space for Northwestern University's School of Medicine. The building expresses the highly technical nature of the modern research laboratory while remaining sympathetic to the collegiate Gothic-style buildings of Northwestern's downtown campus.

The laboratory layout was generated in part by the low floor-to-floor height needed to connect the new building to the north and east. Modular laboratory spaces cluster around vertical chases frequently spaced to minimize the horizontal ceiling ducts. A band of faculty offices and support spaces wraps around the perimeter of the typical laboratory floors. A faculty club occupies the top floor at the southern end of the building. The elevator core is expressed as a strong vertical element in the composition and forms a transition between the entry pavilion and the research tower. The entry lobby on the first floor unifies circulation in the new and existing buildings.

The limestone curtain wall mediates between the adjacent Gothic-style structures and the building's modern expression. The vertical exhaust ducts on the roof are technological elements transformed into modern spires.

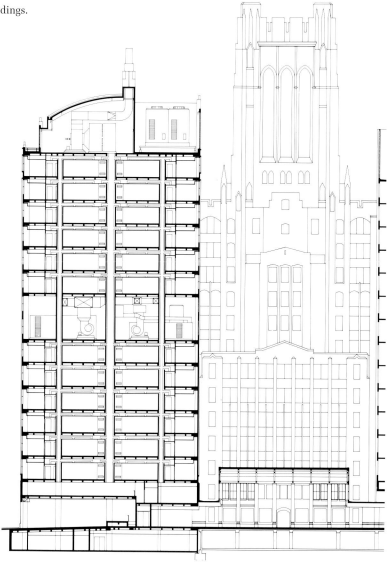

Section

South elevation

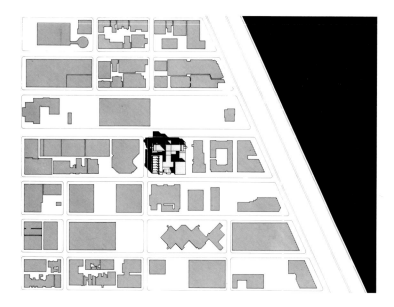

Site plan

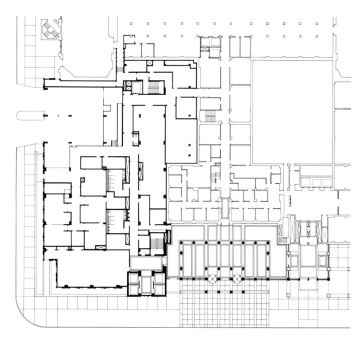

Ground floor plan

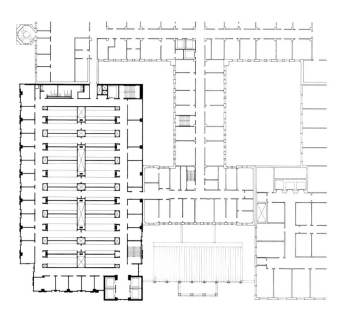

Typical lab plan

Edison Community College, Lely Campus

Naples, Florida 1989

A new satellite campus for the Edison Community College system was to occupy a 50-acre site landscaped with pine groves and palmetto plants common in this region of southern Florida. The complex was to house a library, bookstore, classrooms, laboratories, administrative offices, and dining facilities.

In this proposal, space was carved out of the pine groves to create a site for three parallel classroom bars that form a series of tightly defined, heavily landscaped courtyards.

With the exception of two more figural buildings, the architecture is a backdrop to the lush vegetation. The first building, an entrance pavilion, contains the main entry and an administrative lobby. The second, a sculptural library pavilion, terminates the western end of the main classroom bar and provides a visual focus for the bars. A newly created lake at the campus entrance provides a strong foreground for the entrance and library pavilions.

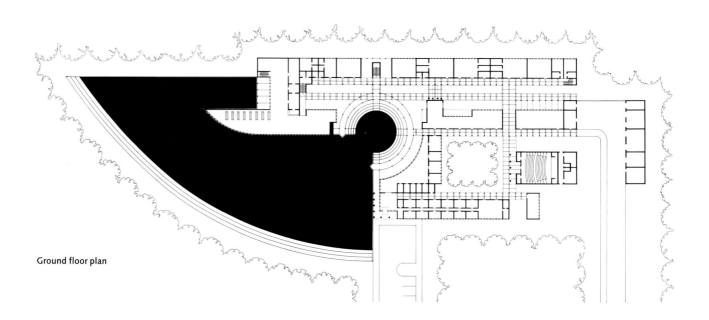

Ground floor plan

Cafeteria and classroom wing

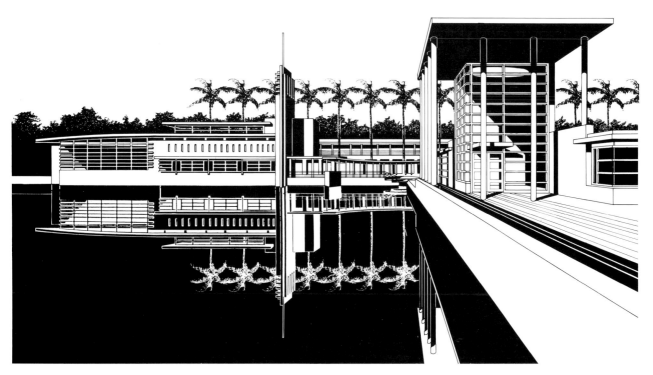

View of entrance

Vernal G. Riffe, Jr. Building

Ohio State University, Columbus 1990–1994

By connecting a pair of existing laboratory buildings, this Biological Sciences Research Building more clearly defines the east edge of campus and forms an entry to the medical school from the south. The building fronts a large intramural athletic field and a heavily traveled pedestrian path between a large dormitory complex and the campus core. Placing the new building between the two existing laboratories unites the three structures into a single composition that creates a strong image for the medical school as one approaches from the north.

The scheme consists of a six-story rectilinear research tower over a two-story base containing shared facilities. The first floor of this base defines the edge of the pedestrian walkway, while the curve of the second-floor reading room wall echoes the horseshoe-shaped football stadium across the athletic field. In the research tower, offices at the perimeter wrap a core of laboratories and mechanical services. Connections to existing research floors provide continuity with the adjacent

buildings. The elevator and lounge core pulls away from the mass of the research tower to provide a transition between the new and existing laboratory blocks. The main lobby is a layered cubic space formed by the wall of the new and existing buildings.

Site plan

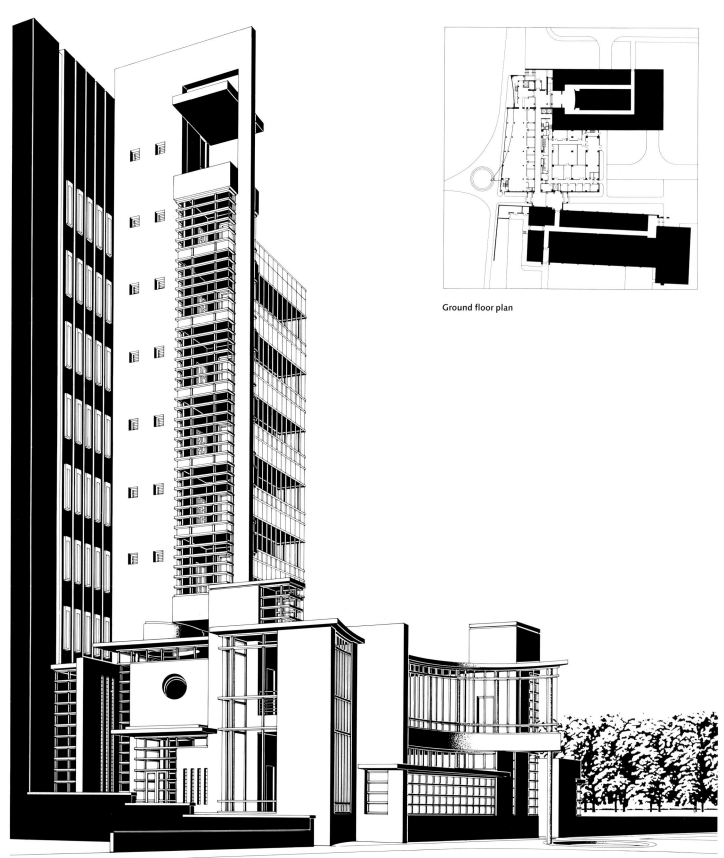

Ground floor plan

View of entrance

CONTINUITY & CIRCUMSTANCE

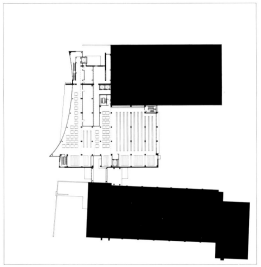

Second floor plan

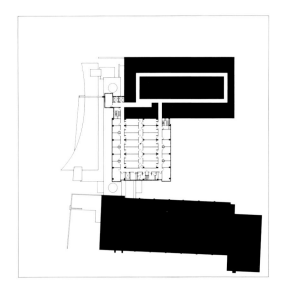

Typical lab plan

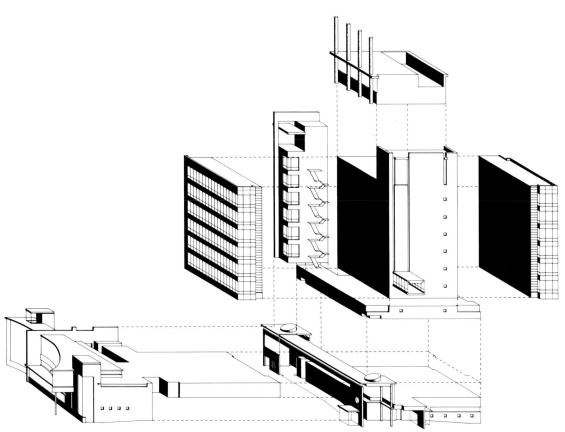

Exploded axonometric

Axonometric

Lobby

Chemical and Life Sciences Building

University of Illinois, Urbana 1990–1996

This teaching laboratory sits at the eastern edge of the University of Illinois campus. Three linear bars, set at right angles to each other, connect two widely separated existing buildings housing the Chemical and Life Sciences departments. By tying the existing buildings together, the new building creates a more defined street edge and formal pedestrian entrance to the campus from the east. The repetitive linear bars accommodate flexible laboratory and office space. The separate auditorium forms a sculptural element in one of the newly created courtyard spaces between the old and new structures.

The facades of the five to seven-story bars are articulated by overlapping layers that distinguish laboratory, corridor, and office functions. A three-story portal punctures the eastern laboratory wall along Goodwin Avenue and acts as a transition to a pedestrian mall that leads to the historic campus core. Flanking this portal are multi-story glazed entrance lobbies for the two departments.

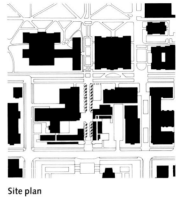

Site plan

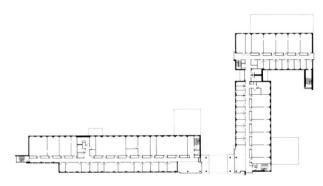

Typical lab plan

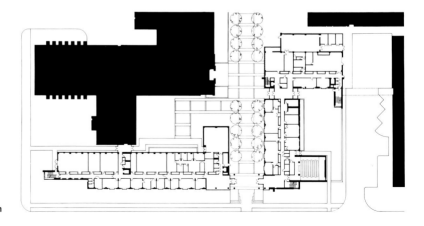

Ground floor plan

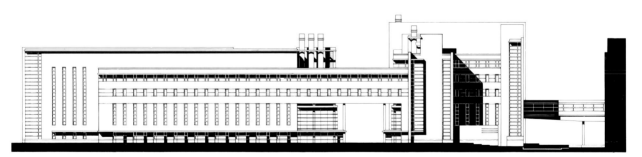

East elevation

Temple Hoyne Buell Hall

University of Illinois, Champaign 1990–1995

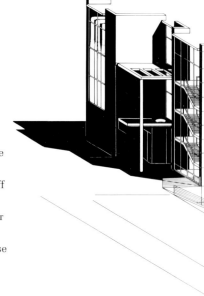

Temple Hoyne Buell Hall will house the graduate schools of Architecture, Landscape Architecture, and Urban Planning of the University of Illinois's Urbana-Champaign campus. The design synthesizes two primary concerns. First, the building's placement and shape should formally interpret the nature of its site at the intersection of the campus's two major axes. The north-south axis derives from the University quadrangle planned by C.H. Blackall in 1905; the military axis was suggested by architect Charles Platt in 1922. Second, the scheme's organization and expression should encourage interdisciplinary teaching between the three schools, which were previously housed in separate buildings.

The resulting scheme consists of four elements that define a multilevel internal courtyard. Two rectilinear volumes housing the loftlike studio spaces define the intersection of the two axes and recall the Georgian-style architecture of many structures on campus, including Platt's 1920s Architecture Building. Two additional lyrical modern buildings are set against the masonry studio volumes. One is a curvilinear bar of glass raised off the ground to allow the courtyard space to penetrate into the interior. The other is a media wall projected off the wall of the north studio volume, designed for indoor and outdoor audio visual presentations. Together these four volumes define an enclosed gathering space that symbolizes this inter-disciplinary building.

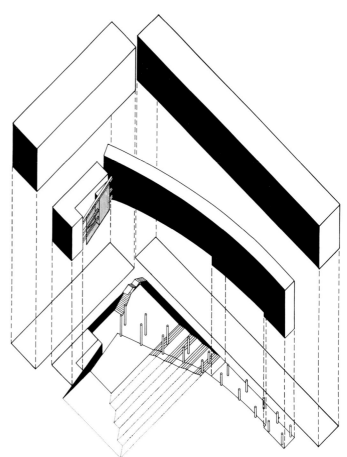

Exploded axonometric

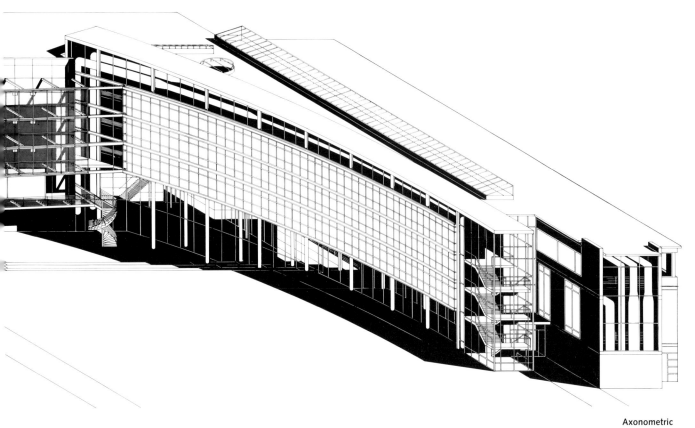

Axonometric

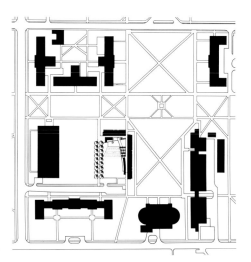

Site plan

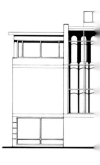

Central space

View of faculty wing

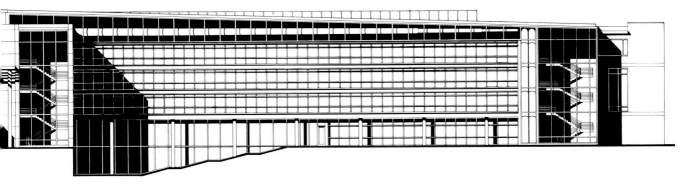

Elevation

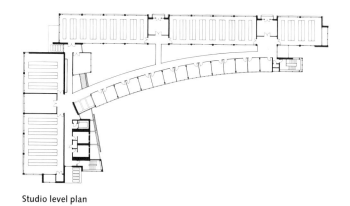

Studio level plan

Ground floor plan

Laboratories and Hospitals TECHNOLOGY & HUMANISM

The design for a modern hospital or laboratory must address spatial relationships, circulation patterns, and technological problems, but human concerns must underlie these pragmatic issues. The hospital's fundamental purpose, after all, is the care of the patient, while the laboratory is a community of scientists for whom nurturing the exchange of information and ideas is as important as the design of the physical structure. Light, space, materials, and form can reinforce technology and suggest human interaction. Concerns for site, culture, and use patterns should alter and enrich circulation and technical services to produce a building that expresses both function and optimism.

The Wyman-Gordon Pavilion at Ingalls Memorial Hospital in Harvey, Illinois responds to the particular care requirements of the psychiatric patient. Here the standard hospital plan of patient rooms lining a double-loaded corridor was transformed into a series of social spaces on an interior street. The public spaces for Scripps Memorial Hospital in Chula Vista, California adapt a standard functional diagram to a specific climate and culture. In the laboratory for Waste Management, Inc. in Geneva, Illinois, office workers' and visitors' environments were as important as the flow of material samples and services. The form of the Dongbu Corporation laboratory in Taejon, Korea responds to the site's open vistas and to the need to create a memorable image for the firm.

Waste Management Environmental Monitoring Laboratory, Geneva, Illinois 1986–1988

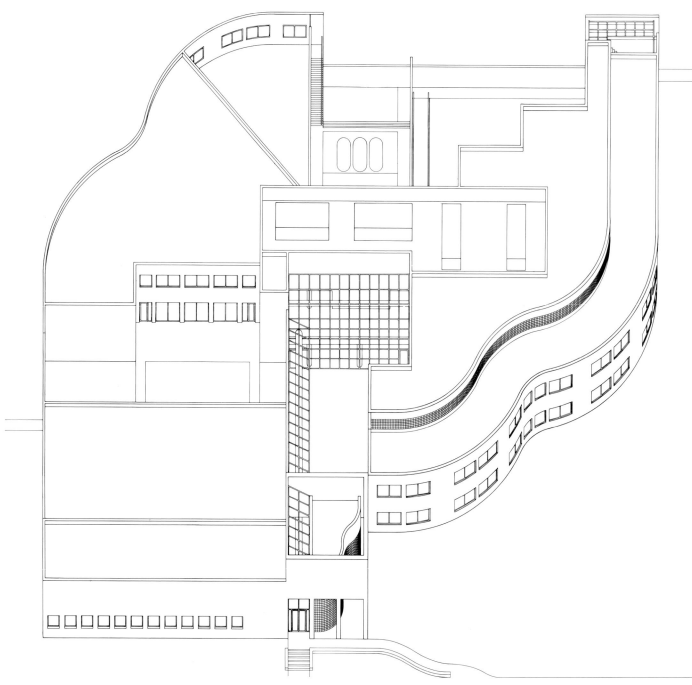

Axonometric

Wyman-Gordon Pavilion

Ingalls Memorial Hospital, Harvey, Illinois 1979–1982

The Wyman-Gordon Pavilion provides three related services to the community: inpatient and outpatient alcoholism treatment programs and an inpatient psychiatric program. The pavilion is sited at the northeast corner of the hospital, adjacent to a residential neighborhood in the southern suburbs of Chicago.

Here the primary goal was to create the noninstitutional, hotel-like environment critical to the success of these particular treatment programs. To achieve this, the project was scaled down into three separate structures for each of the three programs. The arrangement of these elements forms courtyards, some of which are extensions of the inpatient bed units.

The rectilinear outpatient structure forms a street wall facing the residential neighborhood. Entry is through a columnar pavilion attached to this structure. Juxtaposed against the outpatient structure are two, two-story curvilinear inpatient bed units. The space between the curvilinear walls and a rectilinear core of support services forms an internal street with various-sized areas for patient interaction. These important spaces encourage social interchange that promotes a patient's transition to ordinary life.

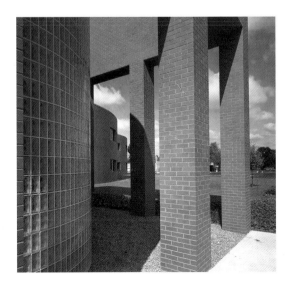

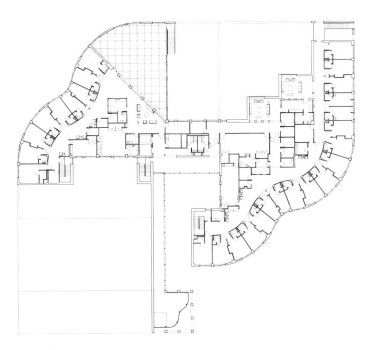

Second floor plan

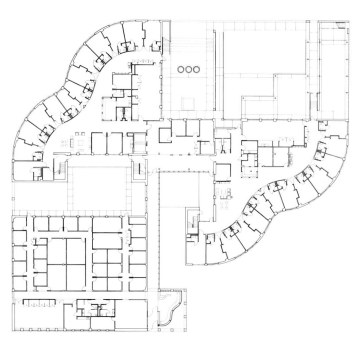

First floor plan

Waste Management Environmental Monitoring Laboratory

Geneva, Illinois 1986–1988

Waste Management, Inc. (now WMX Technologies) wished to build a state-of-the-art facility for collecting and analyzing ground water samples from monitoring wells, chemical treatment plants, and municipal waste sites across the United States. The site is a rural tract of land at the end of the State of Illinois High-Tech Corridor, a concentration of research facilities that stretches west from Chicago.

The building is composed of three parts: laboratories for testing ground water samples from landfills, a general office area, and a service zone for receiving and storing samples and housing mechanical equipment.

A circular masonry screen wall surrounding the mechanical equipment visually anchors the structure to the northwest corner of the site at the intersection of two rural roads. Emanating from this wall is a fanlike structure composed of two laboratory wings bracketing a central, pie-shaped office area. The office overlooks the landfill to the west. The plan responds to circulation patterns for employees, for sample delivery and processing, and for periodic public tours that must be routed to avoid interfering with the analysis process.

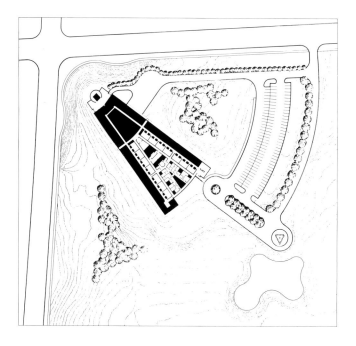

Site plan

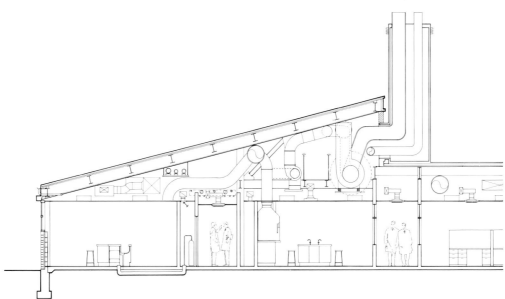

Section at typical laboratory

Scripps Memorial Hospital

Chula Vista, California 1990–1992

This project is an addition to a hospital in a rapidly growing area south of San Diego between a residential neighborhood and a commercial center. It includes a relocated and expanded emergency room, obstetrical services, intensive care units, new medical/surgical and specialty beds, and a main entrance lobby.

A compact two to three-story L-shaped mass contains treatment and patient care spaces. As in the California residential architecture of Rudolph Schindler and Richard Neutra, the building and projecting freestanding walls enclose two courtyards that are exterior extensions of the hospital environment and take advantage of the benign climate. An open stair, a terrace, and an elevator core link the upper floors with a rear courtyard designated for patient use. Patient toilets are expressed on the exterior as a series of stucco and masonry piers that shade the recessed windows of the patient rooms. At the entrance, a floating roof supported at one end by a vertical circulation core shades a series of gardens and ponds extending from the main lobby. This roof form creates a recognizable entry for the entire hospital complex.

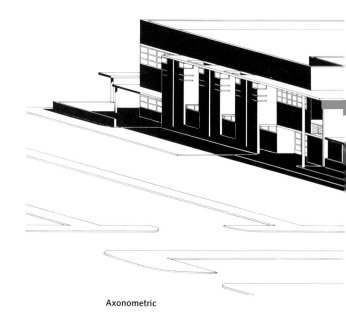

Axonometric

View of entrance

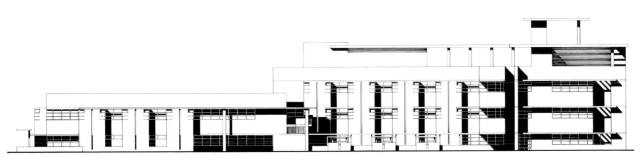

West elevation

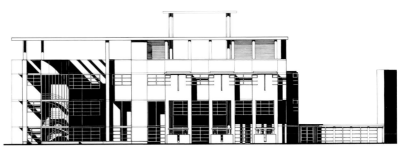

South elevation

Dongbu Central Research Institute

Taejon, Korea 1991–1995

The Central Research Institute for the Dongbu Corporation, a large Korean manufacturer, is located in the Dae Duck Research Park in Taejon, one hundred miles south of Seoul. Sited at a main intersection in the research park, the project contains research laboratories, administrative offices, and a pilot plant for product testing. The building expresses these three programmatic elements in bold forms set against the open vistas of the research park and reflected in an artificial lake in the foreground. A broad arc contains the research laboratories and creates a strong visual identity for Dongbu within the park. A lower pavilion for administrative functions penetrates the research bar at a three-story public lobby. A clerestory loft behind these two elements houses the pilot plant. Each element in the complex can expand independently in a linear fashion. The facility is clad with a metal panel system manufactured by the Dongbu Corporation.

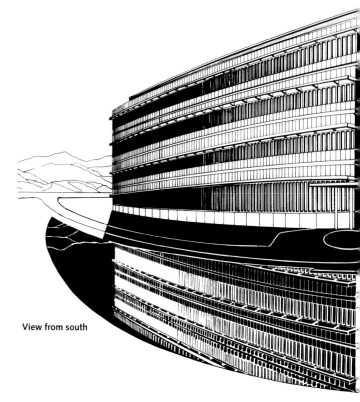

View from south

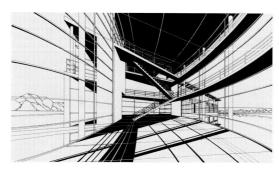

Lobby

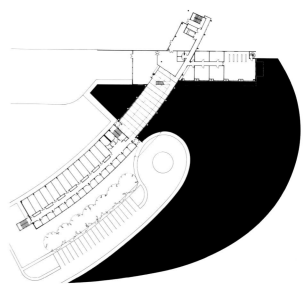

Ground floor plan

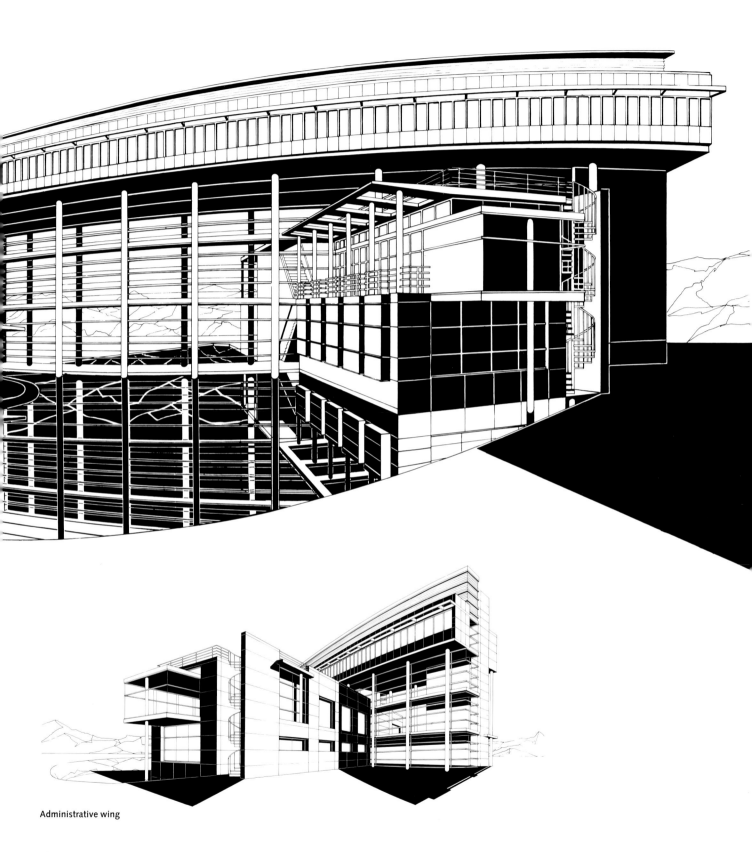

Administrative wing

Airports PLACE & TRANSITION

The growth of air travel in the late twentieth century has changed our perception of time and place. The ability to move across vast areas in relatively short periods of time has compressed our scale of distance and accelerated the pace of cross-cultural exchange; vastly different climates and cultures are now within a few hours' journey. The airport should symbolize this contemporary concept of space and time as well as calm some of the anxiety brought on by rapid change.

Unlike the centrally located railroad station of the nineteenth century, the airport spreads out along a city's undefined perimeter, surrounded by a sea of connecting roadways and parking. The scale of the traditional entry gate or portal must expand to signal arrival. Airport interiors should convey the excitement of arrival or departure. Strongly linked interior spaces can bridge between a specific place and unlimited destinations. The airport must be both a static expression of a particular place and culture and a dynamic expression of transition and movement.

The sweeping ticketing pavilion at the International Terminal at Chicago's O'Hare International Airport establishes a strong land-side image and a gateway presence for the entire airport as seen from the surrounding freeways. Its sequence of interior spaces of varying heights and shapes carved out of the poché of the support spaces provides a strong sense of movement and transition for the arriving or departing passenger. The redevelopment proposed for TWA at John F. Kennedy International Airport in New York extends and reinforces Eero Saarinen's masterpiece terminal, one of the earliest and best examples of expressive airline architecture. The proposed extension increases the terminal's scale without destroying the original spatial integrity of this icon of modern architecture. In the Hong Kong airport proposal, a linear composition links the terminal's arrival spaces to the water's edge, acknowledging the strong relationship between land and water in Hong Kong. The pavilion concept for the Seoul airport was an attempt to mediate between the large-scale requirements of an international airport and the intimate scale of traditional Korean architecture.

International Terminal, O'Hare International Airport, Chicago 1989–1993

International Terminal

O'Hare International Airport, Chicago 1989–1993

The International Terminal accommodates all foreign airline departures and all international arrivals with a 21-gate facility. Three levels contain departure gates, a ticketing pavilion, concessions, support facilities, a train station, and Federal Inspection Services for arriving passengers. Departures are on the upper level, arrivals on the lower level, and baggage handling, mechanical services, and other airline support spaces at the midlevel space at grade.

Sited at the entrance to the airport along a major freeway running east-west, the 800-foot-long arc of the ticketing pavilion establishes a new entry scale and image for the O'Hare complex. The terminal interior is a linear sequence of hierarchically linked, self-contained spaces designed to enhance the sense of movement and transition for the arriving or departing passenger. From the ticketing pavilion on the upper level, a broad corridor flanked by concessions leads west to a central security checkpoint and to the boarding concourse wings. Three shedlike forms on the freeway side at midlevel house the people mover station, which links the terminal to the rest of the airport. Stairs and elevators link this station to the upper-level ticketing hall and lower-level arrival area. The control tower on the runway side acts as a structural fulcrum for both the interior and exterior composition.

The terminal recalls bridges and the airport infrastructure that surrounds the traveler arriving by automobile. It also suggests an aircraft wing with its smooth, taut exterior and skeletal, delicate interior. Ceiling planes are independent of the structural system, alternately engaging and detaching from the structure in sinuous shapes that exaggerate the sense of movement.

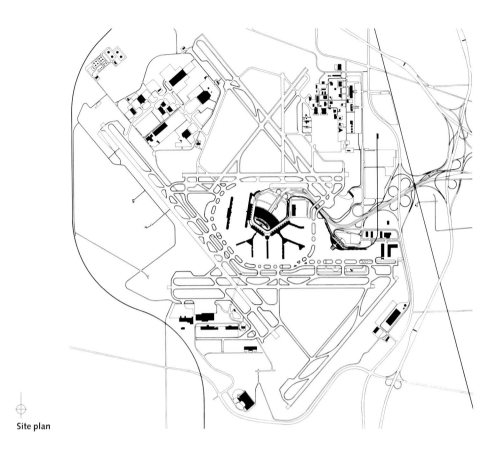

Site plan

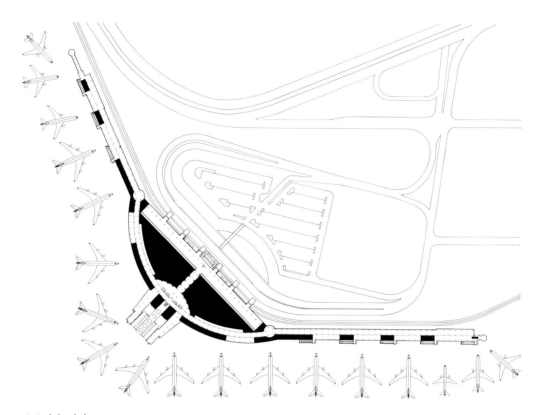

Arrivals level plan

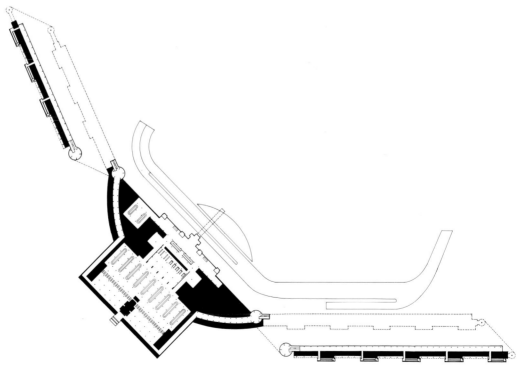

Departure level plan

Departure concourse

Ticketing pavilion

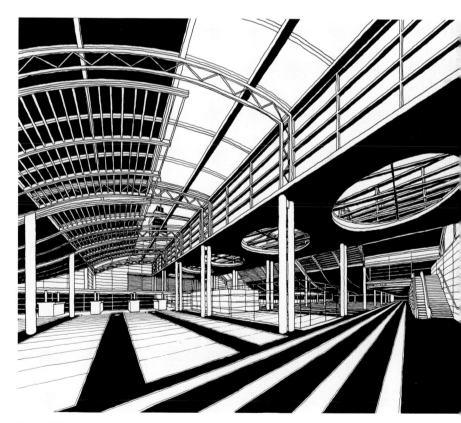

Arrivals hall

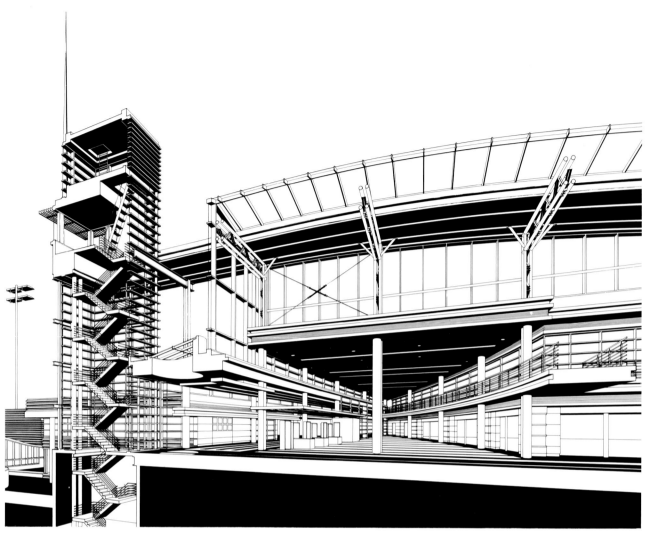

Section perspective at concessions area

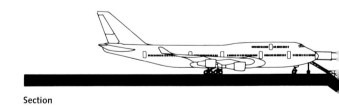

Section

Section perspective at ticketing pavillion

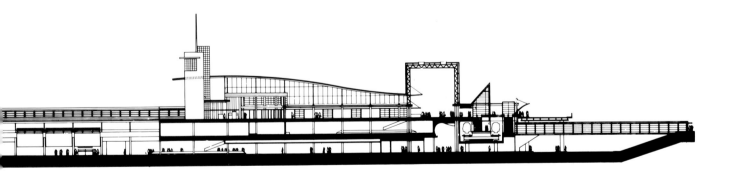

Trans World Airlines Redevelopment

John F. Kennedy International Airport, New York 1989–1990

This project involved the rehabilitation and modification of TWA's Terminals A and B; the expansion of one concourse and the replacement of the other with a new 16-gate concourse; a new underground Federal Inspection Services facility; a meeters-greeters lobby to tie the terminals together; a new roadway behind Terminal A to relieve congested circulation; and other improvements for concessions, security, and baggage handling.

The redevelopment program sought to improve visual and functional cohesion between the two terminals. The character of the two original terminals could not be more disparate. Terminal A, designed by Eero Saarinen and completed in 1962, is a sculptural masterpiece designed to enhance the travel experience through dynamic manipulation of form and space. Terminal B is classic in its use of simple geometric forms. Designed by I.M. Pei for National Airlines and completed in 1970, it currently serves as TWA's domestic terminal. Both create strong memorable spaces that funnel passengers through the various stages of arrival and departure.

This scheme mediates between the rectilinear forms of Terminal B and the curvilinear forms of Terminal A, which are more dynamic in plan and section. The curtain wall of both new structures is primarily glass, the only material common to both existing terminals. The departure roadway and Federal Inspection Services Hall behind Terminal A were depressed one level below grade to maintain the air-side vista from Eero Saarinen's fishbowl waiting space. The new interventions are crystalline backdrops, providing cohesion while maintaining the autonomy of the original terminals.

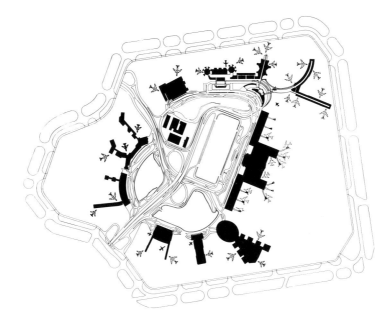

Site plan

Departure concourse looking west

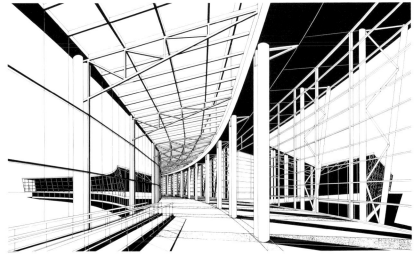

Departure concourse looking east

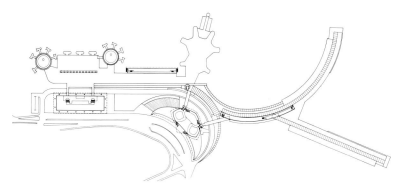

Restaurant level plan

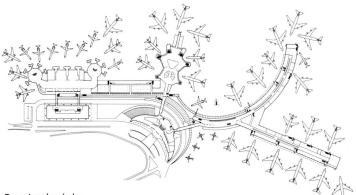

Departure level plan

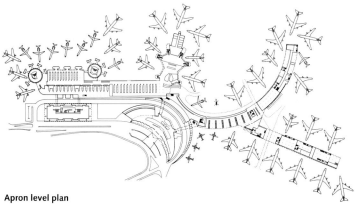

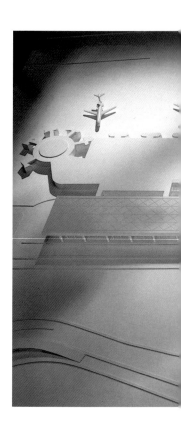

Apron level plan

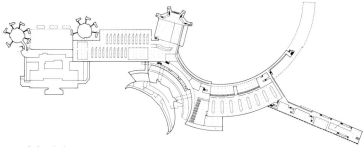

Arrivals level plan

Chek Lap Kok Airport Competition

Hong Kong 1992

Hong Kong's new international airport will be sited on a landfill island northwest of central Hong Kong and linked to the city by rail, boat, and highway extensions. The facility will include 120 departure-arrival gates, a transportation center, hotel, commercial and retail center, and ferry terminal. This scheme was one of eight entries in an invited competition won by Norman Foster & Associates of London.

The scheme proposed terminal and ancillary spaces connected by a centralized people mover station that links the ticketing area, transportation center, waterside ferry terminal, and commercial center. The focal element is the airport terminal building, located between two parallel runways.

It is a unifying element, recognized for its civic importance as a gateway to Hong Kong. Its soaring vaulted ceiling reflects the movement of passengers; high ceilings mark major pedestrian routes and low ceilings define ticketing areas. The terminal concourse is a combined direct access pier and satellite gate facility and was designed as a series of modular components to simplify construction. The new commercial center and harbor terminate the composition and emphasize the importance of water connections to central Hong Kong.

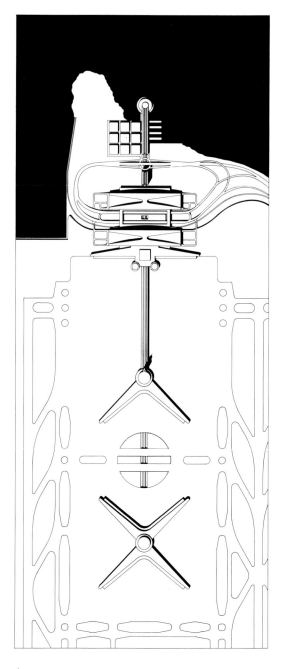

Site plan

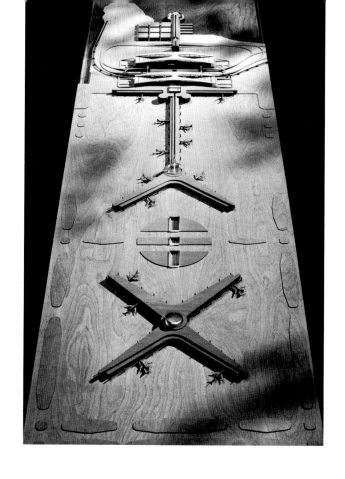

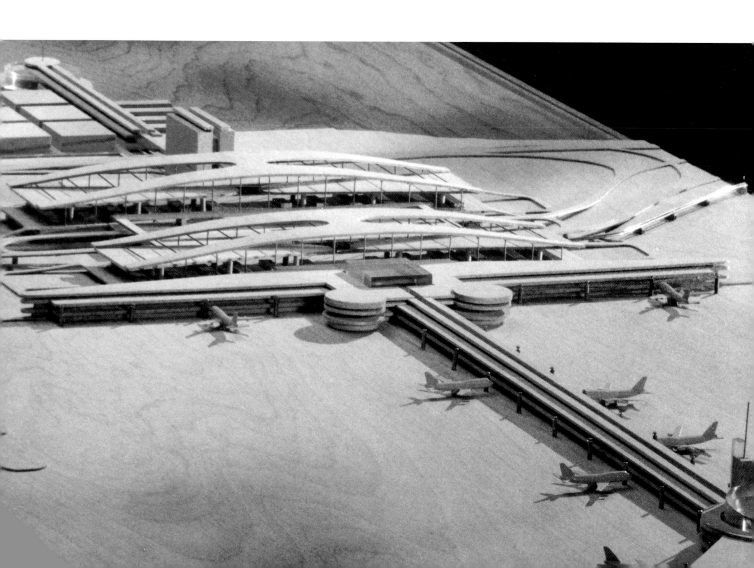

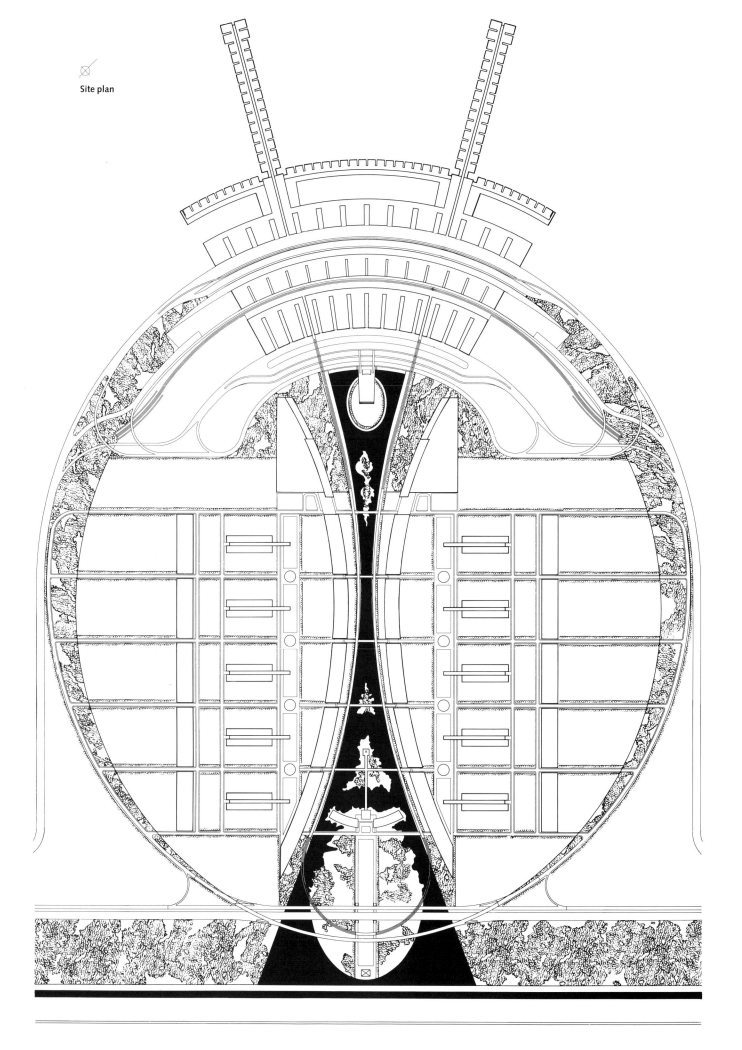

Site plan

The New Seoul Metropolitan Airport Competition

Seoul, Korea 1992

The New Seoul Metropolitan Airport is planned as the hub airport of the Asia-Pacific region. The first phase consists of a 44-gate terminal and concourse. The project also includes an international business center with office, research, retail, recreational, and cultural facilities, as well as hotel and convention facilities.

The terminal buildings were designed as a series of continuous, concentrically curved public spaces. The terminal and concourses are pavilions separated by skylights, which create visual autonomy for the check-in halls and reinforce major circulation routes. The buildings in the international business center reinforce the terminal as the site's focal point. Low retail structures along the central axis adjacent to a park and lagoon create a foreground for the terminal. A landscaped oval ring road unites the business center with the terminal.

Stylistically, the airport appears as a series of linked modular pavilions based generally on the formal elements of traditional Korean architecture: a stone base, a columnar middle section, and a distinctive upturned roof. Courtyards reminiscent of traditional Korean gardens lie between these pavilions.

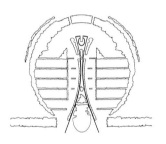

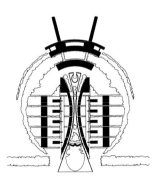

Corporate Office Buildings ICONOGRAPHY & URBANISM

The office tower is the building block of our central cities. In designing these structures the architect is responsible for answering to the client's needs, weighing the demands of context, and addressing the concerns of the broader public. An urban office tower is more than merely an articulated surface enclosing a volume based on economic considerations; the building must also adapt to and complement a specific site and create a strong iconic presence. The standard, commercially viable building should be transformed into something of cultural value.

The successful office tower reads as object against an urban background at three different scales. The building's street-level elements should weave into their immediate surroundings; new exterior and interior spaces should form part of the urban continuum. At an intermediate scale, the building should be neutral; its materials and textures should relate to surrounding structures and streetscapes to provide edge and wall definition. From a distance the building should be a strong symbol for the client and the city. Formal responses to site conditions and to a client's desire to create an image can provide an appropriate backdrop and texture for the late-twentieth-century city.

The Morton International Building in Chicago is a series of interlocking volumes that adapt to specific site conditions to create a new place within the city. Its ground-level spaces form part of the developing series of urban spaces along the Chicago River. The proposed 100 North Wacker Drive tower extended these themes to a site to the east directly across the river. Its position at the intersection of the older city core and the newer developing perimeter gave rise to its formal expression. The Yuksam-Dong Mixed-Use Building in Korea reflects the clash of growth and tradition characteristic of the modern Asian city.

Morton International Building, Chicago 1987–1990

Morton International Building

Chicago 1987–1990

This 36-story high-rise, multi-use building occupies an air-rights site over an operating railroad yard. The site is in the West Loop area of Chicago, bounded by Randolph Street and Washington Street to the north and south, the Chicago River to the east, and a renovated turn-of-the-century warehouse to the west. The program consists of a street-level restaurant, a six-story data center for Illinois Bell Telephone, a parking garage for 435 cars, and a leasable 23-story office tower.

The design responds to the technical challenges inherent in the site and to the desire to create a positive urban intervention. An exterior public arcade and riverside promenade on the building's south side extend pedestrian circulation at street level and lead to stairs that access a public park along the river. The massing is a series of simple, vertically stacked, rectilinear blocks, each housing an individual function. A glazed loggia and vertical clock tower grafted to this stack of blocks give importance to the river edge. These elements represent, in abstract form,

the kinds of traditional architectural features found on many buildings along the Chicago River. A cantilevered suspension truss compensates for unusual foundation conditions at the southwest part of the site and recalls the bridges along the river. The varying floor-to-floor heights, together with patterns created by the vertical structural elements and alternating horizontal bands of gray granite and metal spandrel, produce a richly textured curtain wall.

The lobby continues the theme of asymmetrical overlapping massing with a complex multilevel space entered from the river side. The elevator lobby was raised to mezzanine level to allow the elevator pits to clear the railroad tracks below the building. A sculptural stair provides a transition between the overlapping spaces of the lobby.

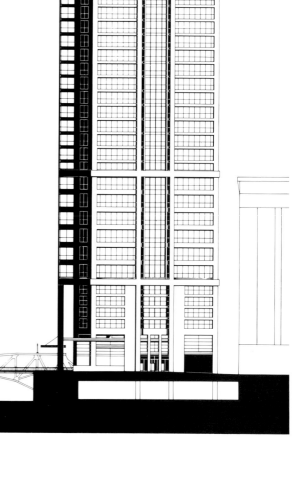

North elevation

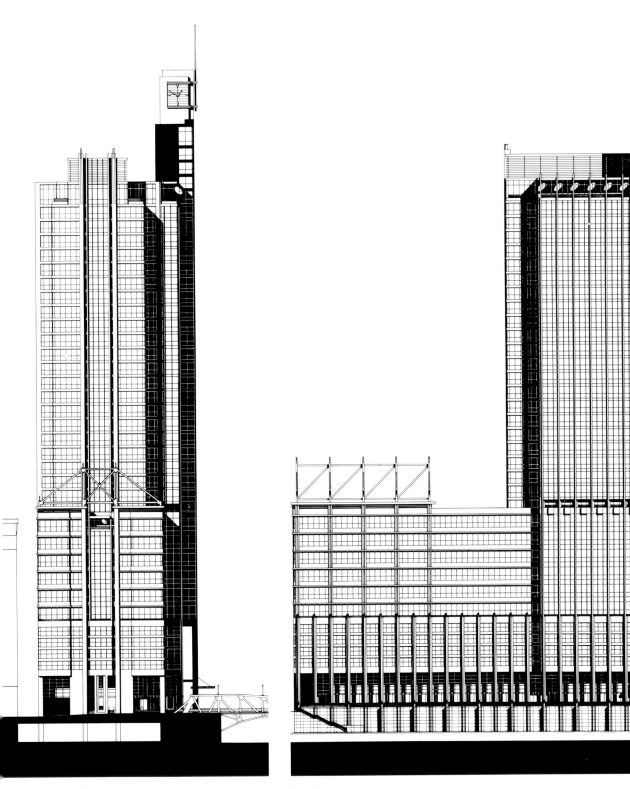

South elevation

East elevation

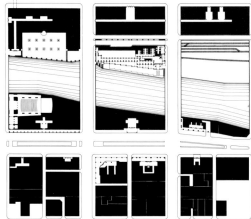

Site plan

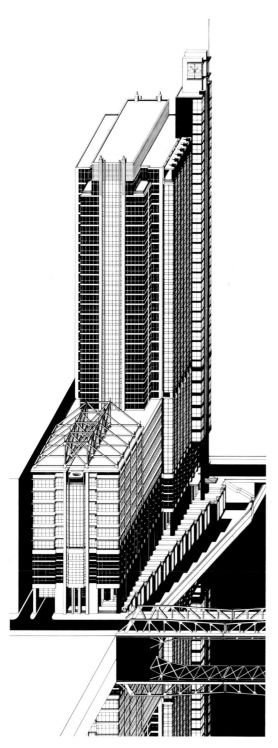

Axonometric

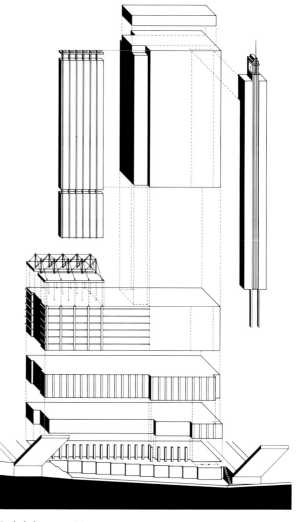

Exploded axonometric

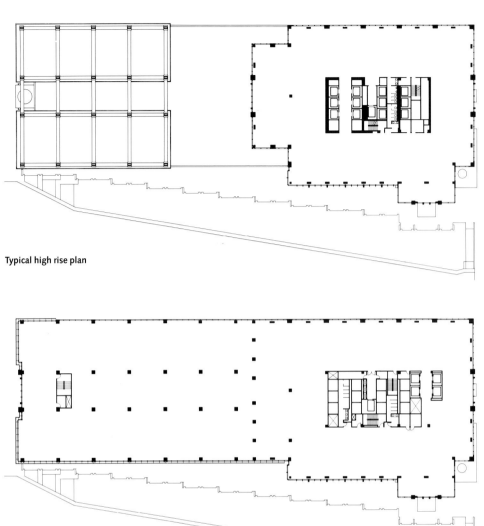

Typical high rise plan

Typical low rise plan

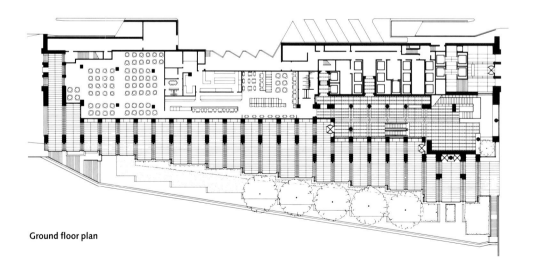

Ground floor plan

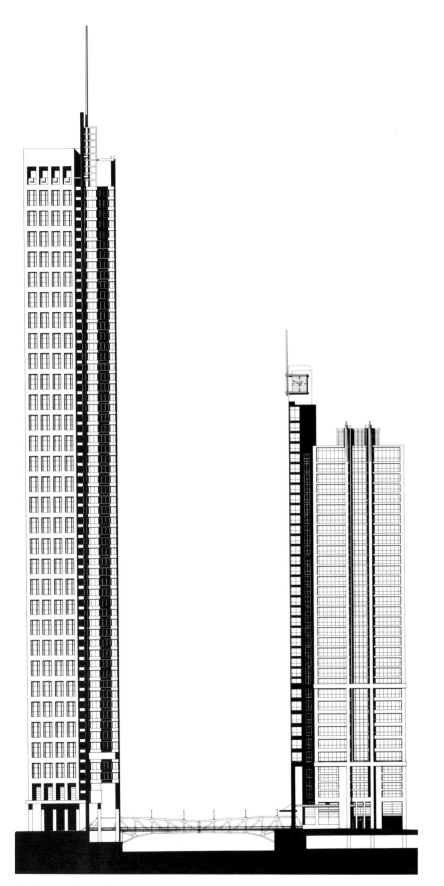

North elevation

100 North Wacker Drive

Chicago 1988–1990

This design for a 64-story office tower, located east of the Chicago River between Washington and Randolph streets on the west edge of Chicago's Loop, proposed a layered composition of slablike elements relating to the local context. The west elevation, facing the river, is a curtain wall of interwoven horizontal and vertical metal and glass bands that recalls the Morton International Building directly across the river to the west.

The east elevation faces the heart of the Loop, where notable turn-of-the-century buildings of the Chicago School of Architecture dominate the urban landscape. This elevation is a stone wall with punched openings; in proportion and scale it defers to the tradition of the historical structures. Between the east and west walls, a black stone slab rises from the lobby to a rooftop penthouse. This large-scale tower was to mark the interface of the traditional downtown core and its evolving western perimeter.

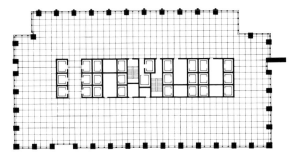

Typical low rise plan

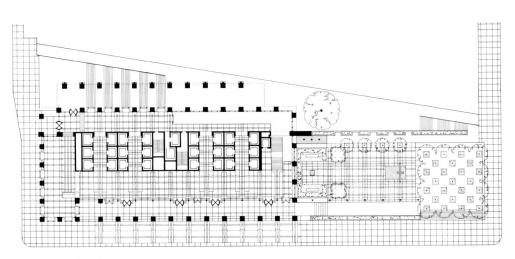

Ground floor plan

Yuksam-Dong Mixed-Use Building

Yuksam-Dong, Kangnam-Ku, Seoul, Korea 1992

This proposal for a 20-story office and department store in a commercial district considers the building's location at a busy intersection. The building's massing both defines the corner and acknowledges the frontality of the longer street elevation. The entrance to the department store in the lower half of the building is through a notched corner accentuated by a sloping electronic billboard. Behind this billboard a multilevel open space connects all floors of the department store. The office floors in the top half of the structure span the longer street elevation; access is through a ground-level lobby. The building's skin clearly distinguishes the two functions. The department store has an expressed structural frame while a taut glass skin wraps the offices above. A rooftop restaurant and terrace terminate the composition.

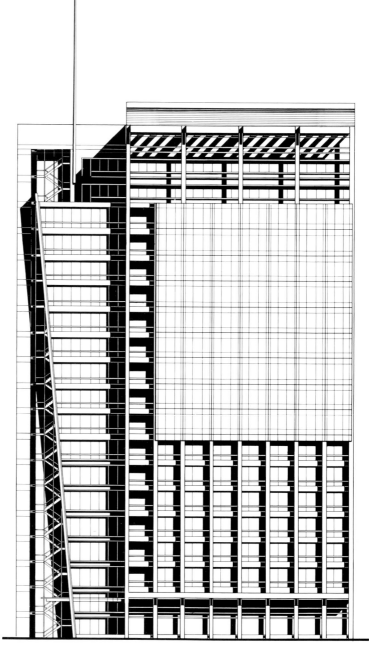

West elevation

Perkins & Will Offices

Chicago 1993

The design for the Chicago offices of Perkins & Will responds to their enclosure, the IBM Building designed by Mies van der Rohe (1971), and to a change in the firm's operating method. The firm wanted a decentralized scheme to replace the hierarchical layout in the previous offices, designed in 1988. The new space encourages close contact between senior and junior staff and allows flexible studio and team groupings.

The office consists of a series of freestanding forms floating within the original gridded Miesian enclosure. These freestanding elements recall the plasticity and planarity of early Mies works, such as

the Barcelona Pavilion of 1929. Glazed or partially glazed offices line a circulation zone adjacent to the building core. The offices are connected by a horizontal plane floating below the ceiling. The work surfaces of the drafting areas interlock with the offices, literally penetrating the office walls. This layered plan allows natural light to reach all work stations and encourages maximum staff interaction.

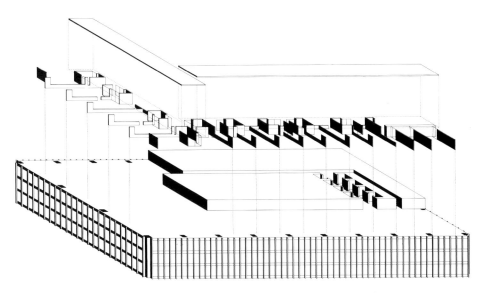

Exploded axonometric

Civic Projects TRADITION & TRANSFORMATION

The architect must reconcile the modern city's past and future. Canonical modern planning theories ignored urban history and dealt instead with purely functional and programmatic criteria. The modernist view was too narrow, but it did enrich our vocabulary. New developments must be seen as continuous comments on the past, though not necessarily expressed with traditional forms. Traditional forms alone cannot respond to modern traffic problems, shifting use patterns, and societal change. There is room in the city for an approach that embraces both innovation and tradition.

Cities consist of superimposed layers of diverse histories. An architect aware of the multiple possible readings of these layers can turn urban complexity and its inherent contradictions into an asset, creating new structures that transform an original site without destroying its positive historical qualities. These new projects must attempt to unify the disparate needs of society into a rich whole.

The competition entry for the Pahlavi National Library in Teheran, Iran explores the notion of the library as a permeable building that maintains the continuity of the city and whose forms are modern responses to climate and tradition. The Orland Park Village Center builds on the traditions of American civic architecture to create a central focus for a suburban Chicago community. The competition entry for the reconstruction of the Navy Pier in Chicago comments on the Pier's transportation history and its relationship to the city. The proposal for redeveloping Alameda Naval Air Station in Alameda, California suggests layering new functions over old to preserve the memory of the former base while ensuring its continued use.

Orland Park Village Center, Orland Park, Illinois 1987–1989

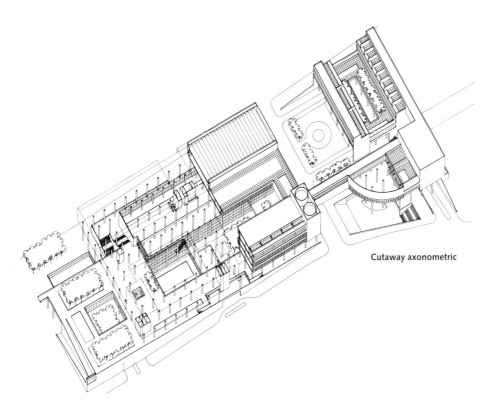

Cutaway axonometric

Section perspective

Pahlavi National Library Competition

Teheran, Iran 1977

This facility was to serve as a major cultural resource for Iran and as part of an international information network. One of the library's most important goals was to promote and direct the development of libraries nationwide. The site was near a large public square envisioned as part of a new town center for Teheran. The project's major elements were a public library, a research library, administrative support spaces, and a center for Iranology that included living spaces for scholars.

This scheme treats the library as a permeable public monument. It provides clear access points and internal circulation while allowing for public circulation through the library gardens. It also connects the urban square with a residential neighborhood to the north. The library's major elements are expressed as individual volumes within the unity of the complex. The research library is on the top floor, under north-lit clerestories, and is raised on pilotis to form an overscaled canopy shading the gardens below. A modern treatment of the layered screens found in traditional Iranian architecture adapts the building to its climate.

Orland Park Village Center

Orland Park, Illinois 1987–1989

Orland Park Village Center provides facilities for local government, a recreation center, and an exhibition hall for a growing suburb southwest of Chicago. The site is on gently rolling land directly west of a large shopping center and a commercial strip along the village's main artery, LaGrange Road. This project refocuses the symbolic center of the village from the shopping center to this new civic complex.

The two major exterior spaces are a formal rectilinear village green and an informal space defined by the retention lake carved into the landscape. Because the village hall faces both spaces and is the physical and symbolic center of the complex, it is the only building with a symmetrical composition. Its massing and placement resolve the axes of a new entry road and the village green. The exhibition hall defines the west edge of the village green and opens onto a terrace overlooking the lake. The recreation center is across the lake, adjacent to a stand of mature trees and softball diamonds. An outdoor amphitheater and covered walkway link the village hall and exhibition building with the recreation center and provide a public gathering spot at the water's edge.

A series of hierarchical forms housing the various functions is the basis of the composition. Assembly spaces have bowed roofs, meeting rooms are cylindrical pavilions, and lobbies and public circulation are expressed as columnar halls. These forms repeat in each of the three buildings and adjust to particular siting conditions. The master plan calls for a theater that will further define the village green. It also suggests a widened entry boulevard to the south, flanked by commercial and retail structures to strengthen the complex's connection to the retail strip.

Site plan

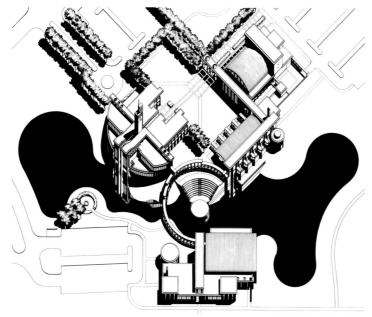

Axonometric

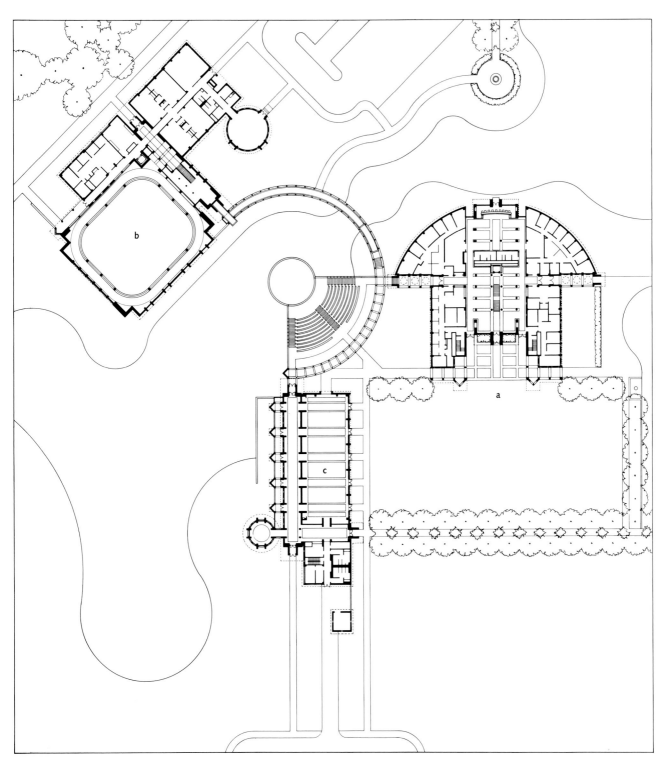

Ground floor plan

a. Village hall

b. Recreation center

c. Exhibition hall

West elevation

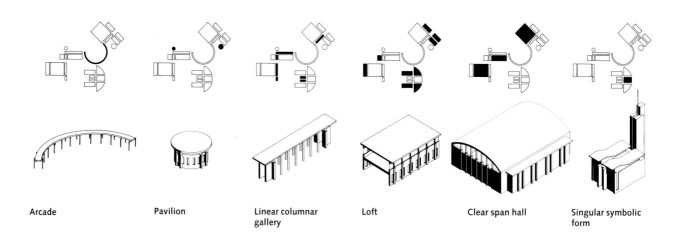

Arcade

Pavilion

Linear columnar gallery

Loft

Clear span hall

Singular symbolic form

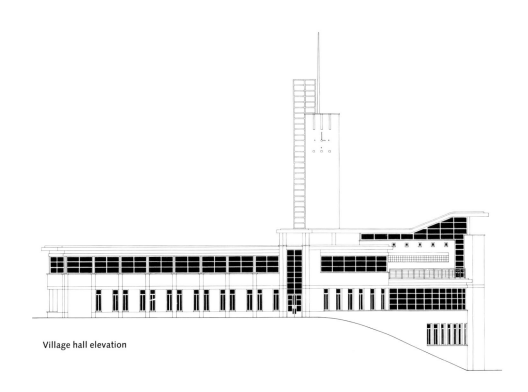

Village hall elevation

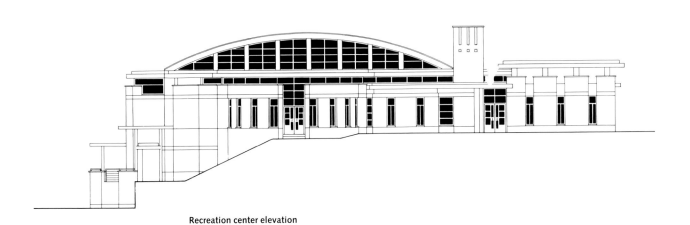

Recreation center elevation

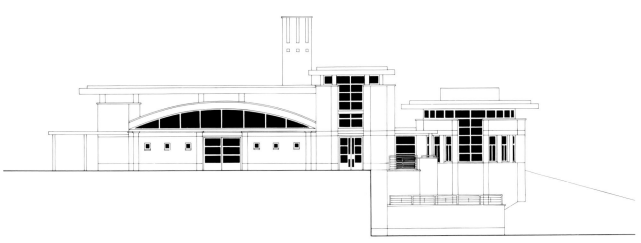

Exhibition hall elevation

TRADITION & TRANSFORMATION

Navy Pier
Reconstruction Program

Chicago 1990

Completed in 1916, Navy Pier was at the time the world's longest pier at over three thousand feet. Designed by Charles Sumner Frost, it served freight and passenger traffic on Lake Michigan from its headhouse, east terminal, and two parallel shed buildings. From the beginning it was also an important site for recreation; eventually this became the pier's sole function. In 1990 the Metropolitan Pier & Exposition Authority sponsored an invited competition to create a recreational and cultural center on the pier that would replace the sheds but restore the original headhouse and terminal building.

This proposal includes an auditorium, exposition hall, winter garden, performing arts hall, hotel, parking, and retail and restaurant space in new and renovated structures. Juxtaposing a crystalline winter garden and an experimental theater against the headhouse formed an arrival plaza at the pier's west end. The broad arc of the new concourse unifies the new and existing elements and forms a backdrop to a stepped open plaza facing the city. It also provides a large civic stage for public events and performances. The arc's radius is anchored at a line formed by extending to the east the center axis of Daniel Burnham's Chicago Plan. This extended axis orients the pier's public spaces to the city's central skyline—a departure from the symmetry of the original sheds—and symbolically expresses the link between water and urban edge that is the essence of Chicago's urban form.

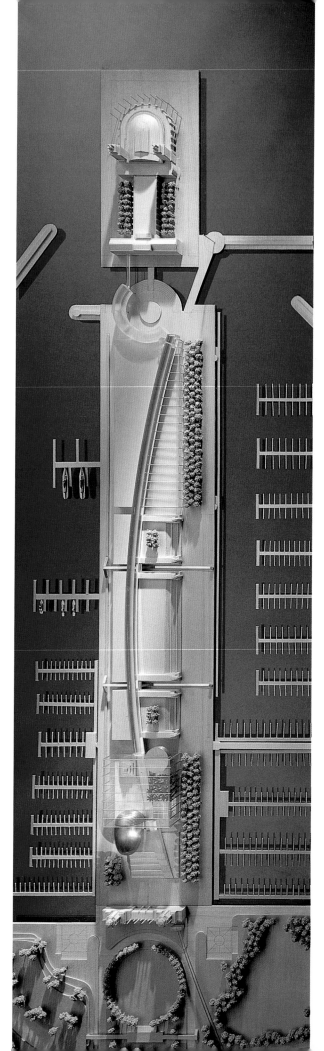

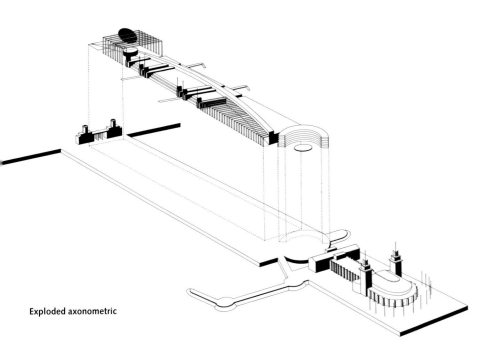

Exploded axonometric

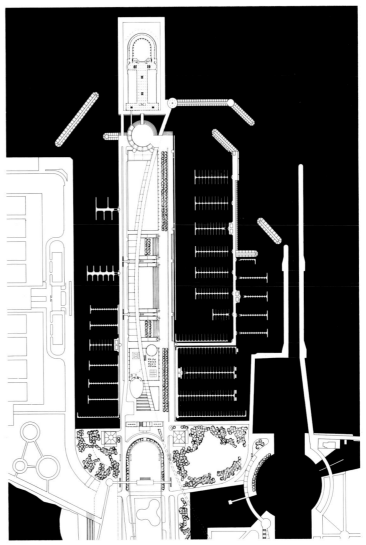

Site plan

Alameda Naval Air Station Redevelopment

Alameda, California 1993

Alameda Naval Air Station occupies a prime waterfront site on a peninsula in the San Francisco Bay near Oakland. The announcement of plans to close the base prompted this study to determine other potential uses for the facility as well as how to maintain traces of its former use.

The base was approached as an urban collage. This scheme retains as many of the existing structures and ordering geometries as possible. New structures were built over or woven into the existing structures to create a tapestry of old and new. A linear structure links the hangars together, incorporating their large-span spaces to house a transportation museum for airplanes, seaplanes, and other vehicles associated with the history of the base. Museum visitors would travel by monorail to remote exhibits along the former runway. A park organized around a transportation theme is an adjunct to the museum.

Spaces for light industry occupy converted repair shops, which are a resource for a new community college career center in the former barracks and officers quarters. New laboratory towers added to the existing maintenance structures create a research and development zone compatible with the facility's educational and industrial components. This zone anchors new commercial and retail development ringing the seaplane harbor. A new residential area to the east would tie the former base to the adjacent community.

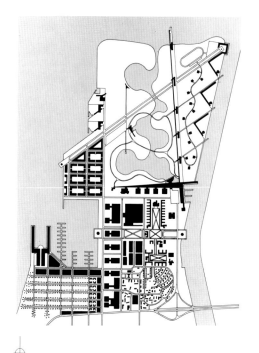

Site plan

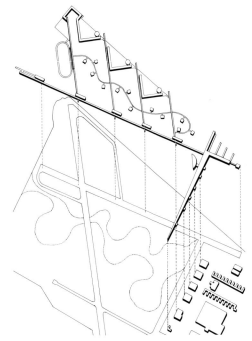

Exploded axonometric

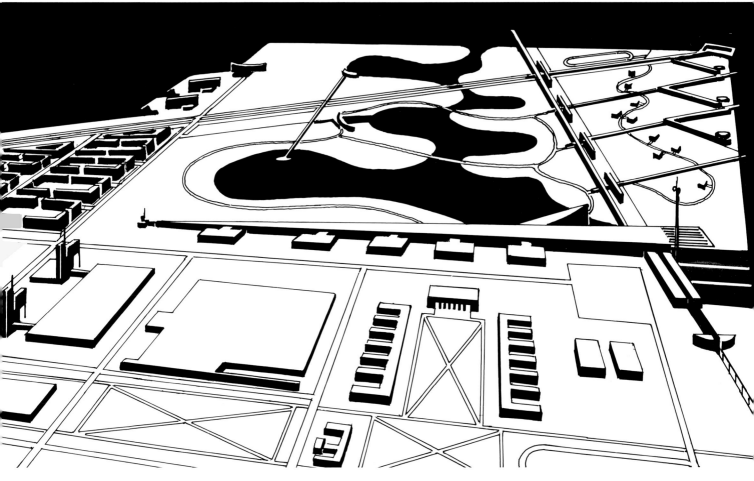

View from south

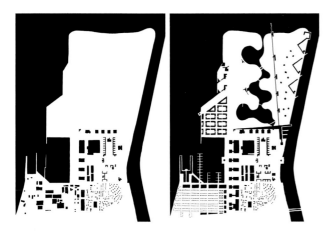

Figure ground studies

West Loop Entertainment District

Chicago 1994

This proposal for a major entertainment district near the heart of downtown Chicago includes a central entertainment attraction, five film studios, a performance arena, five gaming boats, and administrative and support facilities. The proposed site is bounded by Lake Street on the south, Grand Avenue on the north, Halsted Street on the west, and the Chicago River on the east, and presently contains passenger and freight rail yards and warehouse facilities. This solution proposes a vast air-rights development over active rail lines which would act as a bridge between developments in the West Loop and the commercial and retail district surrounding the Merchandise Mart to the north.

The main organizing element is a multilevel interior spine running down Fulton Street from the Chicago River to Halsted Street. The spine connects the studios and the central attraction and terminates at the river's edge with an administrative tower and performance arena, linking the district visually to the center of the city. The riverfront becomes a park where gaming boats are anchored permanently at the shore. The district extends the city grid and would act as a catalyst for peripheral development. The large central hall is surrounded by smaller-scale support facilities that form a transition to the surrounding context.

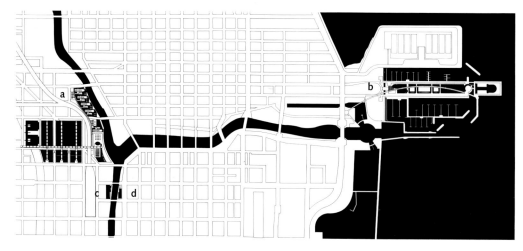

Site plan

a. West Loop project
b. Proposed Navy Pier Redevelopment
c. Morton International Building
d. Proposed 100 North Wacker Drive Building

WEST LOOP ENTERTAINMENT DISTRICT | **193**

Conference Center and Hotel

Beirut, Lebanon 1994–1995

Located along a bend in the Corniche, a boulevard on a cliff fronting the Mediterranean, this project for a 920-room hotel and conference center is a symbol of the cultural and commercial rebirth of Beirut. The complex will be one of the first major public facilities to be built in Beirut since 1975. The design capitalizes on the dramatic site and potential for views of the complex from the city and the Corniche road as one approaches the city from the north.

At the base of the complex, low structures that extend the scale of the city contain public lobbies, hotel support areas, recreational and retail facilities, and restaurants. The base is conceived as a villagelike environment of multilevel plazas, courtyards, and terraces connected by open-air, covered passageways whose materials and scale recall the traditional souks in central Beirut. At the northern end of the base an enclosed passageway connects the hotel lobby with a conference center surrounding an internal courtyard. Arcaded shops line the base along the Corniche road to create a pedestrian promenade along the Mediterranean. Two entry plazas for the hotel and conference center are located off this road, along the eastern edge of the site. A tunnel under the road connects the hotel to a beach club with pools and landscaped terraces carved into natural rock outcroppings. Superimposed on the base at the northwest area of the site is a 52-story hotel tower that acts as a symbolic marker for this prominent location. The adjacent 16-story hotel wing mediates between the tower and the existing buildings along the Corniche road.

View of retail courtyard

Perspective from west

Site plan

Housing COLLECTIVITY & PRIVACY

A dwelling mediates between the individual and the city, between public and private space. The dwelling's public face expresses social structure, while its interior spaces reflect patterns of private living.

Housing forms the texture of our cities. Groups of individual dwelling units form street edges and continuous massing. These edges act as infill, resolving the city's irregular conditions. Urban housing types should reflect the character of their contexts without compromising their individual identity. The exterior of a housing unit should mediate between the building as object and the building as space that defines edge. Interior spaces are a more private world of reflection and personal expression; they should celebrate individual idiosyncrasy. The changing quality of natural light enlivens interior surfaces and reminds us of the natural processes of time. Gardens seen as outdoor rooms extend habitable space to the exterior.

In the Ocean Club complex in Miami Beach, Florida, the dwelling unit is the building block for a larger building mass that responds to a unique context and produces public and private spaces at a variety of scales. The Byucksan Mixed-Use Building in Seoul, Korea varies the shape of housing and office space to adjust to a chaotic urban setting. The proposal for a suburban house in Burr Ridge, Illinois addresses the physical and cultural ambiguity of suburban life, while the progression of interior and exterior spaces in the Nagle-Johnson House in Chicago explores the relationship of old to new.

Suburban House, Burr Ridge, Illinois 1991

Ocean Club

Miami Beach, Florida 1981

This proposal for a mixed-use development in north Miami Beach drew inspiration from the romance and fantasy of the tropical deco hotel architecture of south Miami Beach in the 1930s and 1940s. The program consisted of a 400-room resort hotel, two hundred condominium units, retail space, parking, and a rooftop restaurant and bar on a site between Collins Avenue and the Atlantic Ocean.

Here a base-and-tower typology is sympathetic to the scale of Miami Beach. A 15-story U-shaped hotel facing the ocean approximates the height of the adjacent hotels.

A stepped garden on top of the parking garage forms the setting for a crystalline hotel lobby that projects from the tower into the courtyard. On top of the hotel base is a 35-story tower set back from the ocean and side facades but flush with Collins Avenue. In the spirit of the older hotels, the formal facade faces Collins Avenue while the beach side is more relaxed. A bar and restaurant enclosed in a stepped glazed atrium top the complex, a modernist transformation of the deco rooflines in the South Beach area.

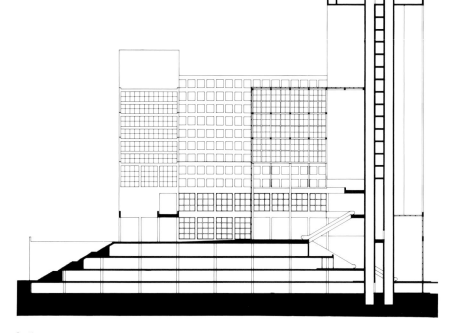

Section

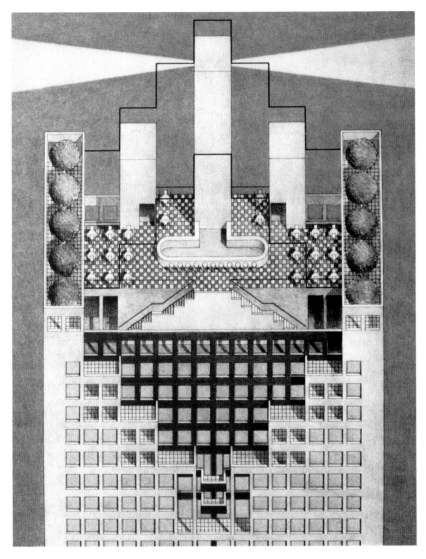

Axonometric

Site plan

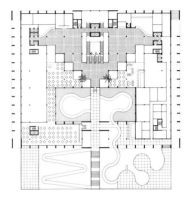

Lobby floor plan

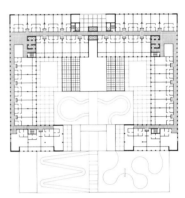

Typical hotel plan

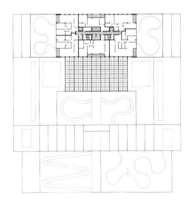

Typical condominium plan

Byucksan Mixed-Use Building

Seoul, Korea 1991–1992

Sited in the Myong-Dong entertainment and shopping district in downtown Seoul, this 30-story high rise houses office and residential units above a base of commercial and retail spaces. Small-scale commercial structures currently occupy this area, but it is undergoing rapid development for higher density use. East of the site is an elevated roadway and a major pedestrian thoroughfare. To the south, an adjacent parcel will be maintained as public open space to guarantee unobstructed views of the hills surrounding Seoul.

In Korean residential planning, residential units typically are oriented toward the best view and exposure to light. Here the curvilinear slabs conform to this strategy. This shape also echoes the curve of the elevated highway and the natural forms of the park to the south. An orthogonal core lines the north side of the building, responding to the rectilinear office structures to the north. A sunken garden, public plaza, and entry lobby relate the building to the pedestrian thoroughfare. A curved electronic billboard terminates the top of the building. The billboard is a gesture to the elevated highway as well as a link to the surrounding entertainment district.

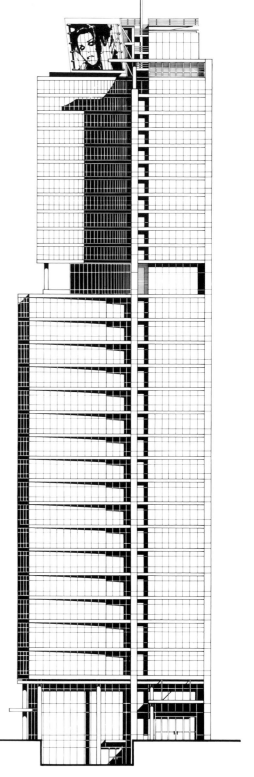

East elevation

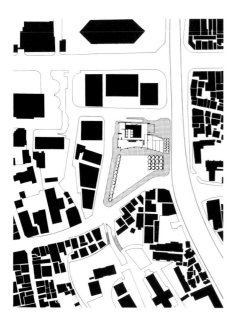

Site plan

View from south

Typical apartment plan

Typical office plan

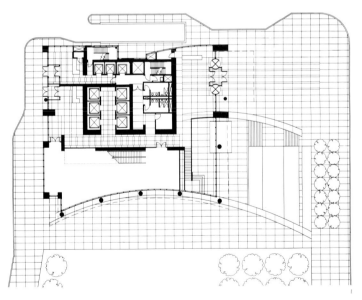

Ground floor plan

Suburban House

Burr Ridge, Illinois 1991

This single-family house is one of a group of eight, each commissioned from a different Chicago architect by a local developer. The developer wished to explore the potential of a hilly wooded parcel of land subdivided into a series of irregularly shaped parcels. The house sits on a lot at the intersection of three roads in the subdivision, adjacent to a creek to the south.

The house is composed of a series of autonomous parts developed from the iconic elements of the traditional suburban home. A base containing a glazed garage and car washing platform celebrates the automobile's integral role in suburban life. A manicured front lawn sits on the roof of the garage. Adjacent to and overlooking this lawn is a transparent prism, a distilled version of the living room picture window. The most public events in the house take place here. Flanking one side of the prism, floating in the trees for privacy, is a steel-trussed structure. On the other side is a towerlike element containing the entry foyer. This tower also accommodates the hedonistic rituals of suburban life: cooking and eating, on the lower level, and exercising, on the rooftop terrace connected to the ground by an exterior spiral stair.

Stone walls define the edges of the site and engage the various glass structures. The fragmented appearance of these walls suggests a ruin, a symbol of the traditional city that spawned the suburbs.

Axonometric from east

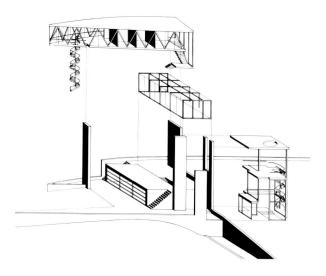

Exploded axonometric

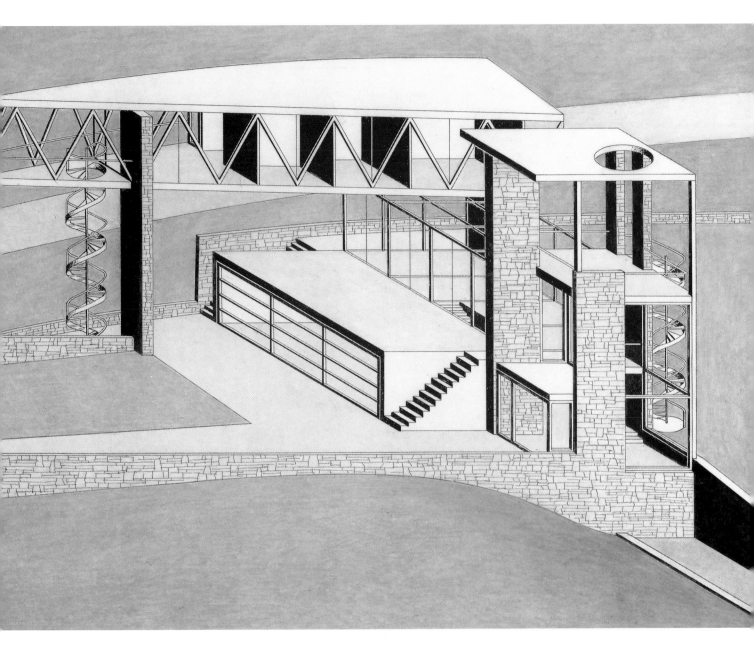

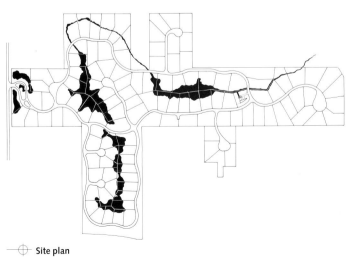

Site plan

View of family room

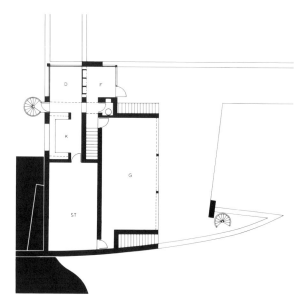

Lower floor plan

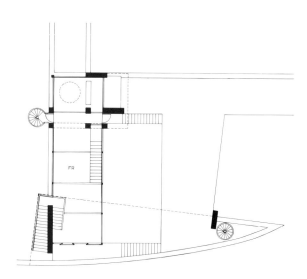

Main floor plan

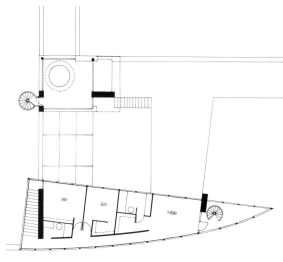

Upper floor plan

View from south

West elevation

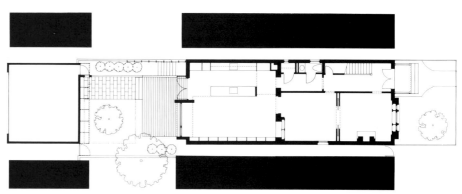

Ground floor plan

COLLECTIVITY & PRIVACY

Nagle-Johnson House

Chicago 1993–1994

This addition to a Victorian home in an older Chicago neighborhood north of downtown transforms the cellular layout of the interior into a sequence of more transparent spaces without destroying the character of the original building. The typical 25' x 125' Chicago lot was approached as a sequence of open spaces that terminates in an outdoor room formed by the west wall of the garage.

The original detailing was maintained and restored while the new spaces are more abstract and planar. Traditional and abstracted trim around openings in the wall of the old house expresses the dichotomy of old and new.

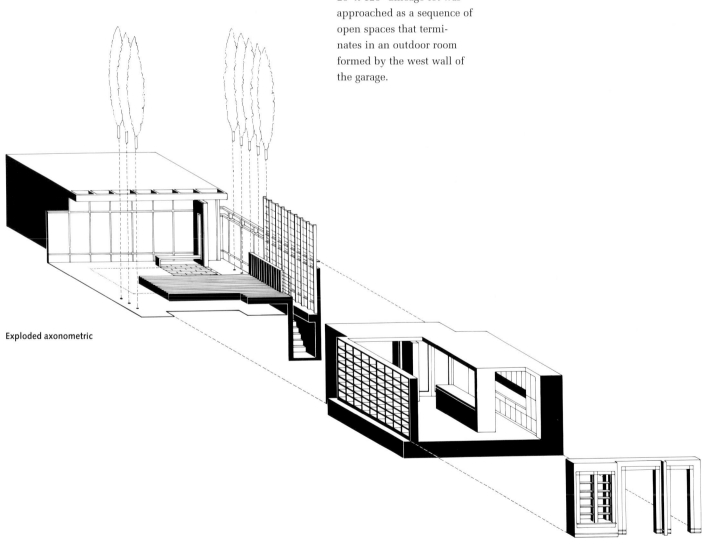

Exploded axonometric

Buildings and Projects

Start date indicates the beginning of conceptual design for built projects or the date when design began for studies or competitions. End date indicates the date of substantial completion for built work. Projects featured in this book are not illustrated here.

1973–1975

**Astronaut Hall Observatory
and Classroom Building**
Cocoa, Florida

Architect: Lemon and Megginson Architects
Client: Brevard Community College
Project Principal: George Megginson
Project Designer: Ralph E. Johnson

1975

**Roosevelt Island
Housing Competition**
New York

Client: Urban Development Corporation
Project Team: Karen Johnson, Ralph E. Johnson

1976

**Biscayne West
New Town Competition**
Miami, Florida

Client: University of Miami
Project Team: Karen Johnson, Ralph E. Johnson

1977

**Pahlavi National Library
Competition**
Teheran, Iran
page 174

Client: The Government of Iran
Project Team: Karen Johnson, Ralph E. Johnson

1978–1982

Woodbridge Middle School
Irvine, California
page 24

Client: Irvine Unified School District
Managing Principal: C. William Brubaker
Design Principal: Ralph E. Johnson
Project Designer: August Battaglia

1978

**Port Saeed
Development Study,
Mixed-Use Development**
Dubai, United Arab Emirates

Client: The Government of Dubai
Managing Principal: Chris Nicholson
Design Principal: Ralph E. Johnson

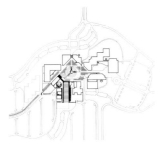

1978–1981

Johnson County Arts and Technology Building
Overland Park, Kansas

Client: Johnson County Community College
Associate Architect: Shaughnessy, Fickel & Scott Architects, Inc.
Managing Principal: C. William Brubaker
Design Principal: Ralph E. Johnson
Project Designer: August Battaglia

1979

Lafayette Square Housing Competition
St. Louis, Missouri

Client: Lafayette Square Corporation
Project Team: August Battaglia, Ralph E. Johnson

1979–1982

Wyman-Gordon Pavilion
Ingalls Memorial Hospital
Harvey, Illinois
page 112

Client: Ingalls Memorial Hospital
Psychiatric Consultant: Dr. Harvey Freed
Managing Principal: Don Richards
Design Principal: Ralph E. Johnson
Project Manager: John Helin
Project Designer: August Battaglia

1979–1982

Pocatello Regional Medical Center Community Hospital
Pocatello, Idaho

Client: Intermountain Health Care, Inc.
Associate Architect: Edwards and Daniels Architects
Managing Principal: Ron Williams
Design Principal: Ralph E. Johnson
Project Planner: Paul Mahajan
Project Team: August Battaglia, John Arzarian, Thomas Demetrion, Dennis Humphries

1981

Al-Mustansiriyah Medical College and Teaching Hospital Competition
Baghdad, Iraq

Client: Mustansiriyah Medical College and Hospital
Managing Principal: Hans Neumann
Design Principal: Ralph E. Johnson, Andrew Mazurek
Project Manager: John Haller
Design Team: August Battaglia, Mark Romack, Thomas Fromm

1981

Ocean Club
Miami Beach, Florida
page 198

Client: Intercorp
Managing Principal: James C. Allen
Design Principal: Ralph E. Johnson
Project Manager: Will Taubert
Design Team: August Battaglia, Mark Romack

1981

Solar-Ray Systems, Inc. Office Building and Warehouse
Peoria, Illinois

Client: Solar-Ray Systems, Inc.
Managing Principal: John E. Nunemaker
Design Principal: Ralph E. Johnson
Project Engineer: Vic Smith
Project Designer: Mark Romack

1981–1982

Brookville Hospital
Brookville, Pennsylvania

Client: Brookville Hospital
Managing Principal: Don Richards
Design Principal: Ralph E. Johnson
Project Manager: John Helin
Project Planner: Andrew Mazurek
Project Designer: Jerry Brown
Job Captain: Mark Hartman

1983

Music Center
Pacific Lutheran University
Tacoma, Washington
page 82

Client: Pacific Lutheran University
Managing Principal: Harry F. Anderson
Design Principal: Ralph E. Johnson
Project Manager: Douglas Tweedie
Project Designer: August Battaglia

1984–1988

Capital High School
Santa Fe, New Mexico
page 26

Client: Santa Fe Public Schools
Associate Architect: Mimbres, Inc.;
Project Architects: Kas Germanas, Sam Jamron
Managing Principal: C. William Brubaker
Design Principal: Ralph E. Johnson
Project Manager: James A. Toya
Project Designer: Elizabeth Fakatselis, Mark Romack, Stuart Royalty

1984–1986

**123 North Wacker Drive
Office Building**
Chicago

Client: Rubloff, Inc.
Managing Principal: James C. Allen
Design Principal: Ralph E. Johnson
Project Manager: Charles Anderson
Project Designer: August Battaglia
Project Team: Mark Romack, Mukhtar Khalil, David Seglin,
Carlos Parilla, Elizabeth Fakatselis, William Schmalz

1985–1988

**Desert View
Elementary School**
Sunland Park, New Mexico
page 32

Client: Gadsden Independent School District
Associate Architect: Mimbres, Inc.;
Project Architects: Kas Germanas, Sam Jamron
Design Principal: Ralph E. Johnson
Project Manager: James Toya
Design Team: Elizabeth Fakatselis, Mark Romack, Jerry Johnson,
Stuart Royalty, Pamela Kurz, Carolyn Smith

1985

**Fifth Street & Locust Street
Parking Garage**
Des Moines, Iowa

Client: City of Des Moines
Managing Principal: James C. Allen
Design Principal: Ralph E. Johnson
Project Manager: Terrence M. Owens
Project Designer: August Battaglia

1986

Metro Center Office Building
Chicago

Client: Rubloff, Inc.
Managing Principal: James C. Allen
Design Principal: Ralph E. Johnson
Project Manager: Charles Anderson
Project Designer: August Battaglia

1986–1988

**Waste Management
Environmental Monitoring
Laboratory**
Geneva, Illinois
page 116

Client: Waste Management, Inc.
Managing Principal: John E. Nunemaker
Design Principal: Ralph E. Johnson
Project Manager: Joseph Schroeder
Project Team: William Schmalz, Andrew Metter

1986–1990

**Tarry Research and
Education Building**
Northwestern University
Chicago
page 86

Client: Northwestern University, Chicago, Illinois
Managing Principal: John E. Nunemaker
Design Principal: Ralph E. Johnson
Interior Design Principal: Neil P. Frankel
Project Manager: James Tworek
Technical Coordinator: Robert Goldstead
Project Designer: Elizabeth Fakatselis
Project Team: Jerry Johnson, Pamela Kurz, Kevin O'Connor,
George Witaszek, Falamak Norzed

1987–1990

**Warsaw Community
High School**
Warsaw, Indiana
page 40

Client: Warsaw Community School District
Associate Architect: The Odle, McGuire & Shook Corporation
Managing Principal: C. William Brubaker
Design Principal: Ralph E. Johnson
Project Manager: James Toya
Project Designer: August Battaglia
Design Team: George Witaszek, Stuart Royalty, Steven Ward,
John Lucero

1987–1989

Orland Park Village Center
Orland Park, Illinois
page 176

Client: Village of Orland Park, Illinois
Managing Principal: Terrence M. Owens
Design Principal: Ralph E. Johnson
Project Manager: Charles Anderson
Project Designer: August Battaglia
Project Team: Carlos Parilla, Carolyn Smith, George Witaszek,
Pamela Kurz, Robin Randall, Steven Ward
Field Team: Thomas Kamis, Ken Kloss

1987–1990

**Morton International Building
100 North Riverside Plaza**
Chicago
page 154

Client: Orix Real Estate Equities
Managing Principal: James C. Allen
Design Principal: Ralph E. Johnson
Project Manager: Charles Anderson
Senior Designer: August Battaglia
Project Designer: Mark Romack
Technical Coordinator: Joseph Pullara
Project Team: Jerry Johnson, John Karabatsos, Stuart Royalty,
Steven Ward, Laura Alberga, Paul Hagle, Carlos Parilla,
Mike Hoffman, Phil Zinny, Eric Spielman

1988–1990

100 North Wacker Drive
Office Building
Chicago
page 166

Client: Rubloff, Inc.
Landscape Architect: Dan Kiley
Managing Principal: James C. Allen
Design Principal: Ralph E. Johnson
Project Manager: Charles Anderson
Project Designer: August Battaglia, Jerry Johnson
Design Team: Gary Jaeger, Paul Wilson

1989–1992

Troy High School
Troy, Michigan
page 44

Client: Troy Public Schools
Managing Principal: C. William Brubaker
Design Principal: Ralph E. Johnson
Project Manager: James Toya
Project Designer: John Arzarian, Jr.
Project Team: Eric Spielman, Mike Hoffman, Geoffrey Brooksher,
Elizabeth Fakatselis, Susan Emmons, Robin Randall,
George Witaszek

1989–1990

Trans World Airlines
Redevelopment
New York
page 144

Client: Port Authority of New York & New Jersey
Managing Principal: James M. Stevenson
Design Principal: Ralph E. Johnson
Project Manager: Jon Pohl
Project Designer: Christopher Groesbeck
Design Team: Mark Jolicoeur, Mark Romack, Jerry Johnson,
Julie Evans, Steven Turckes, Patricia Roberson, Lisa Snow,
Kurt Finfrock

1989–1993

International Terminal,
O'Hare International Airport
Chicago
page 126

Client: City of Chicago, Department of Aviation and Department
of Public Works
Associate Architect: Heard & Associates, Ltd./Consoer
Townsend & Associates
Managing Principal: James M. Stevenson
Design Principal: Ralph E. Johnson
Project Manager: James A. Economos
Senior Designer: August Battaglia
Project Planner: Mark Romack
Project Designer: Elizabeth Fakatselis
Project Team: Joseph Pullara, Jon Pohl, Mike Gillaspie, Mark Jolicoeur
Doug Grimm, Steve Bogay, Robert Ruggles, Dina Griffin,
Paul Pettigrew, Thomas Kamis, Billy Tindel, Larry Robertson,
Paul Hagle, Susan Barnes, Fred Afshari, Michael Poynton,
Henry Lee, Bernie Woytek, Davor Engle, Phil Zinny

1989

Edison Community College
Lely Campus
Naples, Florida
page 94

Client: Edison Community College
Associate Architect: Parker/Mudgett/Smith Architect, Inc.;
Project Principals: Wiley Parker, William Mudgett
Managing Principal: C. William Brubaker
Design Principal: Ralph E. Johnson
Project Designer: John Arzarian
Project Team: Peter Tham, George Witaszek, Carlos Parilla

1990–1996

Chemical and
Life Sciences Building
University of Illinois
Urbana, Illinois
page 102

Client: University of Illinois, Urbana-Champaign/
Capital Development Board
Managing Principal: John E. Nunemaker
Design Principal: Ralph E. Johnson
Project Manager: Thomas Fromm
Project Designer: Ruth Gless
Technical Coordinator: Joseph Chronister
Project Team: Aric Lasher, Julie Evans, Lisa Snow,
George Witaszek, Amy Yurko

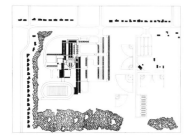

1990–1992

Solon Middle School/
Parkside Elementary School
Solon, Ohio

Client: Solon City School District
Associate Architect: Burgess & Niple, Ltd.;
Project Director: Raymond Bordwell
Managing Principal: C. William Brubaker
Design Principal: Ralph E. Johnson
Project Planner: James Woods
Senior Designer: Ruth Gless
Project Team: Steven Turckes, Gregory Bennett

1990–1992

Scripps Memorial Hospital
Chula Vista, California
page 120

Client: Scripps Memorial Hospital
Associate Architect: James A. Leary Architecture and Planning
Managing Principal: Dewey Schultz
Design Principal: Ralph E. Johnson
Project Manager: Thomas D. Fromm
Project Designer: Christopher Groesbeck
Project Team: Kurt Young-Binter, Wendy Gill

1990–1994

Vernal G. Riffe, Jr. Building
Ohio State University
Columbus, Ohio
page 96

Client: Ohio State University
Associate Architect: Burgess & Niple, Ltd.
Managing Principal: Jeffrey Conroy
Design Principal: Ralph E. Johnson
Project Manager: Chester Turner
Project Architect: Joseph Chronister
Project Designer: Kurt Finfrock, Thomas Mozina

1990

Navy Pier
Reconstruction Program
Chicago
page 188

Client: Metropolitan Pier and Exposition Authority
Managing Principal: Jeffrey Conroy
Design Principal: Ralph E. Johnson
Project Designer: Gengis Yetkin

1990–1995

Perry Community
Education Village
Perry, Ohio
page 52

Client: Perry Local School District
Associate Architect: Burgess & Niple, Ltd.;
Project Director: Raymond Bordwell
Managing Principal: Ralph E. Johnson
Project Manager: James Toya
Technical Coordinator: James Nowak, William Schmalz
Project Designer: August Battaglia, James Woods
Project Team: Eric Spielman, Mike Palmer, Jerry Johnson,
Robin Randall, Robert Ruggles, Celeste Robbins, Carlos Parilla,
Gregory Bennett, Randy Takahashi

1990–1995

Temple Hoyne
Buell Hall
University of Illinois
Champaign, Illinois
page 104

Client: University of Illinois, Urbana-Champaign/Capital
Development Board
Managing Principal: John E. Nunemaker
Design Principal: Ralph E. Johnson
Project Manager: Scott Reed
Technical Coordinator: Robert Gross
Project Designer: Vojo Narancic
Project Team: Steve Turckes, Gary Jaeger, Dean Huspen,
Thomas Vecchio

1990–1991

Aloha Tower
Office Building
Honolulu, Hawaii

Client: Aloha Tower Associates
Developer: The Enterprise Development Co.
Design Principal: Ralph E. Johnson
Project Manager: Charles Anderson
Project Designer: Scott Reed
Project Team: Gary Jaeger, Baek Soo Kim

1991–1995

Dongbu Central
Research Institute
Taejon, Korea
page 122

Client: Dongbu Corporation
Design Principal: Ralph E. Johnson
Managing Principal: Donghoon Han
Project Designers: Gengis Yetkin, Aric Lasher
Project Team: Amy Yurko, Waleed Shalan

1991–1992

Byucksan
Mixed-Use Building
Seoul, Korea
page 200

Client: Byucksan Engineering and Construction Co.
Design Principal: Ralph E. Johnson
Project Manager: Donghoon Han
Project Designer: Aric Lasher

1991

Suburban House
Burr Ridge, Illinois
page 202

Client: Pacific Sakita
Project Designer: Ralph E. Johnson
Model Builder: Kurt Young-Binter

1992

Chek Lap Kok Airport
Competition
Hong Kong
page 148

Client: Hong Kong Provisional Airport Authority
Managing Principal: James M. Stevenson
Design Principal: Ralph E. Johnson
Project Manager: Wally Bissonnette
Project Designer: August Battaglia
Project Planner: Mark Romack, Mark Jolicoeur
Project Team: Gengis Yetkin, Thomas Mozina, Aric Lasher

1992

Yuksam-Dong
Mixed-Use Building
Seoul, Korea
page 168

Client: Dongbu Corporation
Design Principal: Ralph E. Johnson
Project Manager: Donghoon Han
Project Designer: Baek Soo Kim

1992

The New Seoul Metropolitan
Airport Competition
Seoul, Korea
page 150

Client: Korea Airports Authority
Associate Architect: TRA Architects; Samwoo Architects
Managing Principal: James M. Stevenson
Design Principal: Ralph E. Johnson
Project Manager: Wally Bissonnette
Project Designer: August Battaglia
Project Team: Mark Romack, Mark Jolicoeur, Vojo Narancic,
Ruth Gless, Jerry Johnson, Thomas Mozina, Greg Bennett,
Aric Lasher, Paul Pettigrew, Dave Salela

1992

Formica Desk

Client: Formica Corporation
Project Designer: Ralph E. Johnson
Model Builder: Saed Ahmed

1992–1996

The Woodlands High School
The Woodlands, Texas
page 68

Client: Conroe Independent School District
Associate Architect: PBK Architects; Principal: Dan Boggio
Managing Principal: C. William Brubaker
Design Principal: Ralph E. Johnson
Project Manager: Joseph Chronister
Project Designer: Jerry Johnson
Project Team: Steve Roberts, Thomas Mozina, Phillip Kiel,
Carol Siepka, Henry Lee, Susan Broadbent

1992–1995

**North Fort Myers
High School**
Fort Myers, Florida

Client: Lee County School Board
Associate Architect: Parker/Mudgett/Smith Architects, Inc.
Managing Principal: C. William Brubaker
Design Principal: Ralph E. Johnson
Project Manager: James Woods
Project Designer: Jerry Johnson
Project Team: Celeste Robbins, Steve Roberts, Thomas Vecchio

1993

Sambu Office Building
Mapo District
Seoul, Korea

Client: Sambu Construction Company
Design Principal: Ralph E. Johnson
Project Manager: Donghoon Han
Project Designer: Steven Turkes

1993–1994

Nagle-Johnson House
Chicago
page 206

Project Team: Kathleen Nagle, Ralph E. Johnson

1993

**Alameda Naval Air Station
Redevelopment**
Alameda, California
page 190

Client: *Architectural Record*
Design Principal: Ralph E. Johnson

1993–1996

Chelsea High School
Chelsea, Massachusetts
page 74

Client: Chelsea School District
Associate Architect: Symmes Manni McKee Architects;
Project Director: Edward Frenette
Managing Principal: C. William Brubaker
Design Principal: Ralph E. Johnson
Project Director: Ruth Gless
Project Programmer: Raymond Bordwell
Project Team: Steve Roberts, Wendy Gill, Michael Poynton,
Tom Ahleman, Elias Vavaroutsos, Brian Junge

1993

Perkins & Will Offices
Chicago
page 170

Client: Perkins & Will
Design Principals: Ralph E. Johnson, August Battaglia
Project Team: Thomas Mozina, Keith Kreinik, Michael Poynton,
Thomas Peterson, Vicki DeVuono, Pauline Kurtides

1993–1996

Singapore American School
The Woodlands New Town
Singapore
page 78

Client: Singapore American School
Associate Architect: Consultants, Incorporated;
Managing Principal: T.C. Tham
Managing Principal: James C. Allen
Design Principal: Ralph E. Johnson
Project Programmer: James Woods
Senior Designer: August Battaglia
Project Team: Mark Jolicoeur, Celeste Robbins, Thomas Mozina,
Chris Hale, Diane Zabich, Carol Siepka, Susan Broadbent,
Steve Roberts, Joe Pullara, Greg Bennett

1994–1998

**Biomedical Research
Building No. 2**
Philadelphia

Client: University of Pennsylvania
Associate Architect: Francis Cauffman, Foley Hoffman
Architects, Ltd., Neil P. Hoffman, Executive Vice President
Laboratory Planner: GPR Planners Collaborative, Inc.
Managing Principal: John E. Nunemaker
Design Principal: Ralph E. Johnson
Project Manager: Paul Clinch
Project Designer: Jerry Johnson

1994

**West Loop
Entertainment District**
Chicago
page 192

Client: CMC Heartland Partners
Managing Principal: James Allen
Design Principal: Ralph E. Johnson
Project Designers: Steve Turckes, Thomas Mozina

1994–1995

Conference Center and Hotel
Beirut, Lebanon
page 194

Client: Sheraton Hotels
Design Principal: Ralph E. Johnson
Project Director: Walter Hefferman
Senior Designer: Vojo Narancic
Project Team: Kimberly Brown, Nicola Casciato, Brian Junge,
Karla Seelandt, Elias Vavaroutsos

1995–1996

Chicago Academy of Sciences
Chicago

Client: Chicago Academy of Sciences
Design Principal: Ralph E. Johnson
Project Director: Terence M. Owens
Senior Designer: Thomas Mozina
Project Team: Nicola Casciato, Elias Vavaroutsos

Awards

1994 National Honor Award
Troy High School,
American Institute
of Architects

Distinguished Building Award
Perry Community
Education Village,
Chicago Chapter of
the American Institute
of Architects

Distinguished Building Award
International Terminal at
O'Hare International
Airport,
Chicago Chapter of
the American Institute
of Architects

Interior Architecture Award
Offices of Perkins & Will,
Chicago Chapter of
the American Institute
of Architects

Interior Architecture Award
International Terminal at
O'Hare International
Airport,
Chicago Chapter of the
American Institute of
Architects

The Devine Detail Award
International Terminal
at O'Hare International
Airport,
Chicago Chapter of
the American Institute
of Architects

Citation
Perry Community
Education Village,
*The American School
& University*

**The Crow Island School
Citation**
Perry Community
Education Village,
*The American School
& University*

The Shirley Cooper Award
American Association of
School Administrators and
the American Institute of
Architects

1993 National Honor Award
Morton International
Building,
American Institute
of Architects

Honor Award
Perry Community
Education Village,
Cleveland Chapter of
the American Institute
of Architects

Citation
Solon Middle School/
Parkside Elementary School,
*The American School
& University*

Citation
Troy High School,
*The American School
& University*

Distinguished Building Award
Troy High School,
Chicago Chapter of
the American Institute
of Architects

Merit Award
Suburban House,
Chicago Chapter of
the American Institute
of Architects

1992 Honor Award
Solon Middle School/
Parkside Elementary School,
Cleveland Chapter of
the American Institute
of Architects

Honor Award
Warsaw Community
High School,
Indiana Society of
Architects

Distinguished Building Award
Morton International
Building,
Chicago Chapter of
the American Institute
of Architects

**1991 Interior
Architecture Award**
Morton International
Building lobby,
Chicago Chapter of
the American Institute
of Architects

1990 National Honor Award
Capital High School,
American Institute
of Architects

**Selected for the "Emerging
Voices" lecture series,**
Architectural League
of New York

Merit Award
Tarry Research and
Education Building,
Northwestern University,
*The American School
& University*

Distinguished Building Award
Capital High School,
Chicago Chapter of
the American Institute
of Architects

Distinguished Building Award
Waste Management
Environmental Monitoring
Laboratory,
Chicago Chapter of
the American Institute
of Architects

Distinguished Building Award
Orland Park Village Center,
Chicago Chapter of
the American Institute
of Architects

1989 National Honor Award
Desert View
Elementary School,
American Institute
of Architects

Honorable Mention
Desert View
Elementary School,
American Association
of School Administrators

Honorable Mention
Capital High School,
American Association
of School Administrators

Certificate of Merit
Desert View
Elementary School,
American School Board
Association

**1988 Distinguished
Building Award**
Desert View
Elementary School,
Chicago Chapter of
the American Institute
of Architects

1987 Citation
Warsaw High School,
*The American School
& University*

Certificate of Merit
Capital High School,
Association of School
Building Officials

1986 Citation
Capital High School,
*The American School
& University*

**1984 Architectural
Design Award**
Music Center,
Pacific Lutheran University,
Progressive Architecture
Awards Program

**1983 Selected for the
"Young Architects Forum,"**
Architectural League of
New York

Young Architect Award
Chicago Chapter of
the American Institute
of Architects

1982 Honorable Mention
Lafayette Square
Housing Competition

1981 First Place
Al-Mustasiriyah Medical
College and Teaching
Hospital Competition

**1980 Plym
Traveling Fellowship**
The University of Illinois
at Chicago

**1978 Award of Merit for
Unbuilt Architecture**
Quarterback Tower
(Birmingham, Alabama)
Chicago Chapter of
the American Institute
of Architects

Honorable Mention
Pahlavi National Library
Competition

1976 First Place
Biscayne West New Town
Competition

1975 Honorable Mention
Roosevelt Island Housing
Competition

Bibliography

1994 "A Suburban High School Responds to Site Geometries." *Architecture*, March 1994, 39.

"International Terminal, O'Hare International Airport, Chicago." *Habitat Ufficio*, April/May 1994, 44–53.

Linn, Charles. "Form Follows Flight." *Architectural Record*, June 1994, 114–27.

"Troy High School." *Architecture*, May 1994, 111.

1993 Armando, Diego. "El Legado de Dudok." *El Cronista Arquitectura & Diseño* (Buenos Aires), May 1993, 1–2, 8.

Bierman, Lindsay. "International Terminal at O'Hare International Airport." *Architecture*, August 1993, 46–47.

Branch, Mark Alden and Cherly Kent. "Now Arriving." *Progressive Architecture*, June 1993, 88–99

"Byucksan Mixed-Use Building." *Architecture + Interior Design (Korea)*, April 1993, 80–81.

Johnson, Ralph. "Universal, Yet Contextual." *Habitat Ufficio*, April/May 1993, 2.

Kamin, Blair. "O'Hare's New Face." *Chicago Tribune*, May 30, 1993, Section 13, 12–13.

"Morton International Building." *Architecture*, May 1993, 94.

"Morton International Building." *Habitat Ufficio*, April/May 1993, 60–61.

Nesmith, Lynn. "Bioscience/Parks Hall Addition." *Architecture*, March 1993, 33.

"New Architecture School Will Site at Campus Crossroad." *Architectural Record*, June 1993, 21.

"P/A Plans: Schools." *Progressive Architecture*, March 1993, 96–97, 101–2.

Pearson, Cliff. "Urban Collage." *Architectural Record*, October 1993, 100–101.

———. *School Ways: The Planning and Design of America's Schools* (New York: McGraw-Hill, 1993), 84–86, 93–95, 122–25, 156, 179–81.

Stein, Karen. "School Spirit." *Architectural Record*, August 1993, 96–101.

Zukowsky, John. *Chicago Architecture and Design, 1923–1993* (Munich: Prestel Verlag, 1993), 348, 364, 418, 429.

1992 "Architects Series No. 15: Ralph Johnson." *Architecture + Interior Design* (Korea), June 1992, 141–63.

Dibar, Carlos. "La torre Morton de Chicago." *El Cronista Arquitectura & Diseño* (Buenos Aires), December 1992, 1, 7, 8.

Freiman, Ziva. "Neocon 92: Place for Homework." *Progressive Architecture*, August 1992, 14.

"Morton International Building." *A+U*, April 1992, 118–26.

1991 Bruegmann, Robert. "Local Asymmetries." *Inland Architect*, March/April 1991, 43–49.

———. "The Rationalist Tradition." *Inland Architect*, March/April 1991, 50–53.

"Chicago Eight Design Model Houses." *Architecture*, December 1991, 25.

Dixon, John Morris. "Confident Times Revisited." *Progressive Architecture*, July 1991, 94–99.

"Dongbu Central Research Institute." *Architecture + Interior Design (Korea)*, November 1991, 48–49.

Gapp, Paul. "A Brawny Chicagoan, Design of Morton International Building Accomplishes Daring Feats." *Chicago Tribune*, September 22, 1991, Section 6, 20.

Nereim, Anders. "A Cathedral of Learning." *Architectural Record*, January 1991, 68–71.

Pearson, Clifford. "Prairie Tech." *Architectural Record*, January 1991, 94–97.

"Perry Community Education Village." *Architecture*, January 1991, 27.

"Waste Management Environmental Monitoring Laboratory." *Architecture*, July 1991, 85.

1990 Fisher, Thomas. "The Place of Government." *Progressive Architecture*, October 1990, 65–77.

"International Terminal at O'Hare Airport." *Metropolitan Review*, May/June 1990, 66–73.

Phillips, Alan. "WMI Environmental Monitoring Laboratory." *The Best in Industrial Architecture* (New York: Watson-Guptill Publications, 1990), 112–13.

Saliga, Pauline, ed. *The Sky's the Limit: A Century of Chicago Skyscrapers* (New York: Rizzoli International Publications, 1990), 270–71, 292.

Stucch, Silvano. "Riverside School in Sunland Park, New Mexico." *L'industria delle costruzioni*, 32–37.

1989 "123 North Wacker Drive, 100 North Riverside Plaza." *Bauwelt*, October 1989, 1930–35.

"Desert View Elementary School, Santa Fe High School, Perry Community Education Village." *Metropolitan Review*, September/October 1989, 90–99.

Fisher, Thomas. "Presenting Ideas." *Progressive Architecture*, June 1989, 89, 91.

———. "Desert High." *Progressive Architecture*, August 1989, 78–81.

Tigerman, Stanley. *Chicago Architecture in the New Zeitgeist: In Search of Closure* (Lisbon: Fundacão Calouste Gulbenkian, 1989), 106–7.

"100 N. Riverside Plaza, Chicago, Illinois." *The Chicago Architectural Journal 8* (1989): 186–87.

Johnson, Ralph. "Crow Island School." *Metropolitan Review*, November/December 1989, 48–49.

Johnson, Ralph. "Type, Program & Place: Four Projects." *University of Tennessee Journal of Architecture II* (1989): 34–39.

1988 "123 Wacker Drive." *Metropolitan Review*, January/February 1988, 40–41.

"100 North Riverside Plaza." *Metropolitan Review*, Summer 1988, 88–91.

"A Civic Complex, Orland Park, Illinois." *The Chicago Architectural Journal 7* (1988): 176–77.

"Combining High-Tech and De Stijl in a New Office Tower." *Interiors*, May 1988, 78.

Dillon, David. "Contrasting Pair of El Paso Schools." *Architecture,* August 1988, 78–80.

Freeman, Alan. "A Tale of Four New Towers and What They Tell Us of Trends." *Architecture,* May 1988, 125–31.

"In Progress (100 Riverside, Orland Park)." *Progressive Architecture,* July 1988, 37, 41.

"Inventive Regionalism Sparks a Prototype for the Desert." *Architectural Record,* September 1988, 106–9.

"A Kit of Indigenous Design Parts." *Architectural Record,* December 1988, 101.

Pastier, John. "Skyscraper Revolution and Evolution." *Design Quarterly 140* (1988): 20–21.

Solomon, Richard Jay. "The Familiar Face of 123 North Wacker." *Inland Architect,* May/June 1988, 49–53.

1987 "The 1987 Esquire Register." *Esquire,* December 1987, 106.

"Office Building Hotel Complex, Chicago, Illinois." *The Chicago Architectural Journal 6* (1987): 102–3.

The Chicago Architecture Annual, 1987 (Chicago: Metropolitan Press Publications, 1987), 208–19. (123 North Wacker Drive, Waste Management Environmental Monitoring Laboratory, Desert View Elementary School, Tarry Research and Education Building, Warsaw Community High School)

Dumaine, Brian. "Architects for the 1990's." *Fortune,* June 22, 1987, 159.

Gapp, Paul. "As Classy as 123, New Building Enhances Wacker-Franklin Strip." *Chicago Tribune,* February 15, 1987, Section 13, 10.

1986 Burkhardt, Francois. *Lieux? De travail* (Paris: Centre Georges Pompidou, 1986), 22–23.

The Chicago Architecture Annual, 1986 (Chicago: Metropolitan Press Publications, 1986), 214–19. (Music Center, Pacific Lutheran University; Capital High School)

1985 *The Chicago Architectural Journal 5* (1985): 150–51. (Capital High School)

The Chicago Architecture Annual, 1985 (Chicago: Metropolitan Press Publications, 1985), 186–95. (Fifth Street & Locust Street Parking Garage)

Conroy, Connie. "The Next Generation: Work by Young Architects." *Inland Architect,* November/December 1985, 35.

"Office Building, Chicago, Illinois." *Progressive Architecture,* February 1985, 47.

"Pflegeeinheiten in Krankenhausern," *Baumeister,* February 1985, 60.

1984 "Die neuen Wolkenkratzer in den U.S.A." *Baumeister,* February, 1984, 55.

"Ingalls Memorial Hospital, Wyman-Gordon Pavilion." *A+U,* May 1984, 91–97.

The Chicago Architectural Journal 4 (1984): 88. (123 North Wacker Drive)

"Modernism: Is It Still Alive." *Inland Architect,* May/June 1984, 17.

"Music Center Pacific Lutheran University." *Progressive Architecture: 31st Annual P/A Awards,* January 1984, 88–91.

"Worlds Fair Charrettes: A Look at Concepts for 1992." *Inland Architect,* March/April 1984, 46.

1983 "Académie du Musique, Pacific Lutheran University." *L'architecture d'aujourd'hui,* October 1983, XLII–XLIII.

"Architecture and the Museum." *Inland Architect,* March/April 1983, 27.

Bruegmann, Robert. "Little Journeys to the Offices of Architects." *Inland Architect,* May/June 1983, 28.

Dietsch, Deborah. "A Degree of Design Innovation on Campus." *Interiors,* December 1983, 32.

"A Hybrid Hospital and Home." *Architectural Record,* June 1983, 98–101.

Globota, Ante. *Chicago, 150 Years of Architecture, 1833–1983* (Paris: Paris Art Center, 1983), 185–86, 231, 236.

The Chicago Architectural Journal 3 (1983): 60, 109. (Music Center, Pacific Lutheran University)

1982 Boudaille, Georges. *Biennale de Paris section architecture 1982: La modernite ou l'esprit du temps* (Paris: Editions L'Equerre, 1982), 201.

"Brookville Hospital." *The Chicago Architectural Journal 2* (1982): 90–91.

"Chicago: La griglia l'infinito." *Domus,* March 1982, 23.

"Corporate Headquarters for Solar-Ray Systems, Inc." *A+U,* August 1982, 110–11.

Johnson, Ralph. "Solar Ray Headquarters." *Threshold 1: The Journal of the Chicago School of Architecture,* The University of Illinois at Chicago (1982): 12–14.

"Les nouveaux gratte-ciel Américains: la cinquième génération," *L'Architecture d'Aujourd'hui,* April 1982, 75.

"Pluralism's Poses." *Inland Architect,* July/August 1982, 38.

"Recent High Rise Building in U.S.A." *A+U,* October 1982, 101.

"Winners of the Journal's Architectural Drawings Contest." *AIA Journal,* September 1982, 37.

Zukowsky, John. "Drawings and Architect's Biographies." in *Chicago Architects Design* (New York: Rizzoli International Publications, 1982), 158–59. (Ocean Club)

1981 "Exhibition of Work by Members of the Chicago Architectural Club." *The Chicago Architectural Journal 1* (1981): 81.

1978 Gapp, Paul. "Iran Honors Chicagoan for His Library Design." *Chicago Tribune,* June 18, 1978, Section 6, 6.

"Pahlavi National Library." *Domus,* August 1978, 21.

"Pahlavi National Library." *Progressive Architecture,* June 1978, 21.

1976 Markham, Wayne. "A New Town Downtown." *The Miami Herald,* May 30, 1976, Section K, 1.

"Midwesterner Wins Biscayne West Competition." *Progressive Architecture,* August 1976, 19.

1975 "Crises in Housing." *Architectural Record,* November 1975, 112.

Nevins, Deborah. *The Roosevelt Island Housing Competition* (New York: The Architectural League of New York and Wittenbunn Art Books, 1975), 21.

Illustration Credits

Numbers in roman refer to page numbers. Numbers in italics refer to illustration numbers.

Mark Ballog
© Steinkamp/Ballogg Chicago: 147 (top)

Orlando Cabanban: *18*, 166, 210 (middle and bottom), 211

Chicago Historical Society: *2 (neg. HB-29509 0)*

David Clifton: 206

Aurelio Galfetti: *14*

Harr © Hedrick-Blessing: 54

© Hedrick Blessing: *11*, 113–15,

Ralph E. Johnson: *9*

© Karant & Associates, Inc., Barbara Karant: 211

Balthazar Korab, Ltd.: 48–49 (top), 51

Leon Krier: *17*

© George Lambros Photography: 111, 116–19

Marco Lorenzetti
© Korab/Hedrick Blessing: 170–71

Dennis McClendon: *1*

Nick Merrick © Hedrick Blessing: Title page, 45–47, 48 bottom, 49 bottom, 50, 52, 56–58, 60–67, 125–28, 130–33, 136–37, 140–41, 143, 153, 156–57, 159–61, 163-65, 173, 177–180, 184–87, 210 (top)

Greg Murphey: 26–31, 40, 42–43, 81, 88–89, 91–93

Robert Reck ©: 23, 33–34, 37–39

Shimer © Hedrick Blessing: 149

James Steinkamp
© Steinkamp/Ballogg Chicago: *24, 25*, 71 (both), 96, 103, 105, 147 (bottom), 151, 188, 192–93, 196, 218

Livio Vacchini: *12, 13*